Housing and Homelessness

Sophie Watson with
Helen Austerberry

Housing and Homelessness
A FEMINIST PERSPECTIVE

ROUTLEDGE & KEGAN PAUL
London, Boston and Henley

First published in 1986
by Routledge & Kegan Paul plc

14 Leicester Square, London WC2H 7PH, England

9 Park Street, Boston, Mass. 02108, USA and

Broadway House, Newtown Road,
Henley on Thames, Oxon RG9 1EN, England

Set in Century Schoolbook
by Inforum Ltd, Portsmouth
and printed and bound in Great Britain
by T.J. Press (Padstow) Ltd,
Padstow, Cornwall

Library of Congress Cataloging in Publication Data

Watson, Sophie.

Housing and homelessness.
Bibliography: p.
Includes index.
1. Homelessness—Great Britain—History.
2. Homeless women—Great Britain—History. 3. Women,
Poor—Great Britain—Dwellings. 4. Housing policy—
Great Britain. I. Austerberry, Helen. II. Title.
HV4545.A3W38 1986 362.8'3 85–14281
British Library CIP data also available

ISBN 0–7102–0400–0

Contents

Contents

Preface and acknowledgments

This book marks a personal turning-point. For six years Helen Austerberry and I worked together as feminists involved in housing and homelessness. Since the beginning of this year we have gone our separate ways, Helen to work with a feminist architects' collective and to train as a homoeopath, and myself, to Australia to continue working on women and housing issues. I wrote this book initially as a PhD thesis which was submitted to the Open University in December 1983. I am indebted to Helen for doing half the interviews with homeless women, on which the second part of this book is based. It was a long and sometimes difficult process, made possible and enjoyable by the fact that it was shared. Together also we constructed the questionnaire and coded the information for computer analysis. For these practical contributions, for shared ideas, for her support and friendship throughout the period of working together I am most grateful.

For the interviews we were dependent on contacting homeless women through hostels and advice agencies. In this, the After Six (now Housing Advice Switchboard) collective, Mrs Bruce, Elizabeth Carruthers, Helen Daniels, Wendy Massey and Mrs Smith were most helpful. To the homeless women themselves who shared their lives and experiences with us, we are especially indebted. Without them this book would not have been possible. I would also like to thank Anna Davin for pointing me in the right direction with the early historical material, Adah Kay and Charles Legg for their very constructive input, Stephen Merrett for helpful comments on several chapters and Jan Wells for improving the final manuscript. Philip Sarre supervised the thesis at the Open University giving encouragement and valuable suggestions along the way. I was fortunate in having Linda

McDowell and Alan Murie examine the thesis, with whom I had a most interesting and helpful discussion at the oral exam. Susan Craig, Wanda Dziubinski, Eve Hussey, Carol Johns, Michelle Kent, typed the manuscript at various stages and I thank them all both for the typing and for their interest in the text. Others who contributed with their friendship and support include John Allen, Linn Cameron, Allan Cochrane, Jos Cornwell, Jane Deighton, Tony Eardley, Jenny Earle, Sally Gilbert, Russell Hay, Alexi Marmot, Doreen Massey and Ruthie Petrie. My father's keen eye and red pen helped improve the final text and I thank him for this. More important, both my parents – Dorothy Watson and Graham Watson – have been consistently positive and encouraging about my work for many years and I would like them to know how much I appreciate it.

Finally, there are two people without whom this book may never have been written. In 1980 when Helen and I left Homeless Action to do this research, it was Michael Edwards' and Kerry Schott's encouragement, support and practical help that got us started. Despite their busy lives they continued to be a source of very great support, from finding us offices and grants to giving sharp and critical comments on the thesis when they were most needed. For this, and more, Helen and I thank them both.

Sophie Watson
Canberra, May 1984

Abbreviations

CSO Central Statistical Office
DE   Department of Employment
DOE   Department of the Environment
DHSS Department of Health and Social Security
GLC   Greater London Council
LBA   London Boroughs Association
MHLG Ministry of Housing and Local Government
NAB   National Assistance Board
OPCS Office of Population and Census Surveys
SBC   Supplementary Benefits Commission

PART I

Chapter 1

Introduction

Houses are not simply bricks and mortar. They play a central part in how we live our lives. This book explores the role of housing from a new perspective: the part housing plays in affirming and reproducing the traditional nuclear family and women's role within it; the definition of housing need or homelessness from a feminist perspective; the impact of the absence of a house or home on the satisfaction of an individual's needs and women's survival in the housing market. We look at the way British society in particular (and western society in general) defines and creates housing 'needs', at the way housing is provided and allocated to exclude specific forms of household, and at the experiences of a particular group – single women – upon whom these processes have profound impact.

Houses, then, do not simply represent a form of shelter: in addition they embody the dominant ideology of a society and reflect the way in which that society is organized. In Britain, the dominant social relations are both patriarchal and capitalist: men have greater economic and social power than women and workers are exploited for profits to be made. Consequently the form in which housing is produced, the means by which it is financed and the way in which it is allocated reflect the division of labour both within the labour process and between the sexes. For example, the organization of domestic labour and childcare is individualized and largely the work of women, rather than collectivized in the public sphere, and this is incorporated into the way houses and estates are designed and constructed.

Two themes underlie the argument. The first is that British housing policy and the housing market operate in favour of the traditional nuclear family household. Moreover, this dominant family model assumes a domestic role for women, such that the housing system acts to positively reinforce women's subordinate economic and social status. An important consequence of this centrality of the family to housing is the marginalization of all other forms of households, in particular single-person households. One way of trying to understand both women's relation to housing and the role of housing in reproducing the traditional family is to analyse the processes by which women become marginalized in the housing sphere. The lived experience of this exclusion can throw a sharp light on how these patriarchal family relations are created and maintained. It is for this reason that the experiences of single homeless women are a central focus of this book.

There is every indication that housing need is growing amongst single people. This derives from their being on the margins in the housing market. We need first to clarify what is meant in this book by 'single women' or 'single-person household', since the term 'single' presents problems. 'Single' is generally used to denote both 'not being married' and 'never having been married'; and sometimes to denote 'being alone' without involving any assumption about marital status. In relation to housing the last of these definitions is for us the crucial one. Since housing policy tends to be oriented towards the family household, and in the public sector more specifically towards households with children, an individual who currently has responsibility for dependent children will have greater access to public housing than someone who has no such responsibility. Marital status as such has no relevance: it may have an impact on an individual's current housing situation for historical reasons, but for single people who are in search of housing, current marital status is irrelevant. A single woman is thus defined here as a woman who is not living with a spouse/cohabitee/children but wants to leave or is forced to leave this situation in the near future. Under this rubric, therefore, are women who are divorced or separated, or women who have children in care, adult children or children for whom they are not responsible as well as women who have never cohabited, married or had children. It is interesting that there is no specific term which adequately describes this expanded notion of 'single'; this in itself is an indication of the lack of recognition attributed to it.

4

The case for recognition of the growing housing needs of single households is complex. If there is nowhere for someone to go, his/her housing need or homelessness is rarely expressed in terms of demand. Instead, people who are unable to amass the financial and social resources necessary to enter the housing market may be forced to accept intolerable living conditions, overcrowding in shared accommodation, or domestic violence, simply because of lack of alternatives. We define such homelessness or housing need as 'concealed'. Nevertheless a comparison of the level of housing provision for single people, and for single women in particular, against the changing demographic patterns, substantiates the argument that the concealed housing need amongst these groups is growing. Traditionally, the private-rented sector has provided the major source of housing for single people. Its decline from 34 per cent of the stock in 1961 to 13 per cent in 1981 (CSO, 1983, p.114) clearly had implications for single households. For example, in the 'never married' under thirty age group, Holmans (1983, p.22) calculated that the proportion of men and women in privately rented accommodation had fallen from 72 per cent in 1977 to 53 per cent in 1981, and from 66 per cent in 1977 to 53 per cent in 1981 for men and women respectively. In the second place, special local authority schemes for single people have been severely affected by the recent cuts in overall expenditure on housing. This situation worsened by a decrease in the number of beds in large hostels and lodging houses over the last few decades. Indeed, there are only 760 bedspaces for women in direct-access hostels in London, compared with over 6,000 bedspaces for men (Austerberry and Watson, 1982). Of course, such accommodation offers no real solution for single people, but any option is better than no option at all.

Demographic data on the other hand shows an increase of 989,590 (30 per cent) in the number of one-person households (living as such) between 1971 and 1981 (Census, 1981, p.xii). One reason for this is the increase in the number of households of men and women who have never married. Calculations of headship rates based on data from the Census and the labour force survey (Holmans, 1983) show an increase in headship rates among never-married men and women in all age groups from 1961 to 1981. The greatest increase in household formation rates of never married men and women is in the 20–24 age group which is accounted for by the trend towards marriage at a later age (for both partners). In 1980 the median age at marriage was 23.1 years for women, 25.6 years for men, compared with 22 years and 24 years respectively in 1971 (CSO, 1983, p. 29). There is also a decrease in the overall marriage rate, with a smaller proportion of the population entering marriage at any stage of life. Another factor in the rising number of single households is the increase in the breakdown of marriages and cohabiting relationships (although accurate figures on the latter are difficult to obtain). In the United Kingdom the total number of divorces granted rose from 27,000 in 1961 to 157,000 in 1981 (CSO, 1981, p.31). There has also been a substantial increase in the number of elderly single-person households. In 1961 there were 1,193,000 one person households over retirement age which accounted for 7 per cent of all households. By 1981 there were 2,770,670 one-pensioner households, roughly 14 per cent of all households (OPCS, 1983, p.xiv). This demographic shift has particular implications for women: in the sixty-five and over age group the male to female ratio is approximately 3:5 (CSO, 1983, p.13). Moreover, the proportion of elderly people living alone is higher for women (over half of whom, in the seventy-five and over age group, live alone) than for men.

This apparent imbalance between single women's housing need and provision introduces the second line of enquiry in this book: the effects of this lack of provision for women. Does women's homelessness or housing need become concealed? If so, are there differences between the women who resort to hostels and the women who find other temporary housing solutions, or do they all constitute a relatively homogeneous group who could be termed 'homeless women'? Do some women remain in intolerable or unsatisfactory domestic situations because of a lack of available alternatives? Can housing situations that a woman herself defines as inadequate or intolerable constitute homelessness? Indeed, is it possible to define 'homelessness' at all when the notion of a 'home' in the context of a patriarchal and capitalist society involves specific values?

An essential theme to our discussion is that homelessness must be analysed in the context of the specific social and economic conditions of the time. We argue that perceptions and definitions of homelessness have important implications for

6

explanations of homelessness and for the nature of provision and policy towards the defined homeless population, as well as toward those not so defined. The research into homelessness in the 1960s and 1970s with its almost exclusive focus on homeless families, single men and young people, has been weakened by its failure to grapple adequately with the problems of conceptualization and definition. The design of our research into the experiences of 160 single homeless women in London, on which the second half of the book is based, was intended specifically to address these shortcomings.

In the case of single-person homelessness, particularly single and female homelessness, the need to shift the focus from the individual to an analysis of wider social and economic structures is especially important. An adequate framework must first analyse the marginality of single housing provision and the increasing numbers of single-person households; and second, explain how patriarchal social relations, the sexual division of labour and the dominant family model in a capitalist society all serve to marginalize women in the housing sphere. It is on such a framework that this book is based.

Chapter 2

Definitions of homelessness

An essential starting point is the construction of a workable definition of homelessness and the specification of an appropriate sample of homeless women. There is remarkably little consensus among policy makers, researchers, local authorities and voluntary housing organizations as to a definition of 'homelessness', although the meaning attributed to it has important implications for quantification, policy and provision, and for any explanation of its cause. Only a minority of writers (Greve *et al.*, 1971; Brandon, 1974) have raised the issue; others have presented a definition with no theoretical explanation, or assumed a meaning for the term, without giving any definition at all. As Brandon wrote (1974, p.5):

> How can the researcher begin to define it . . . writers have used it in almost every conceivable way – from meaning complete shelterlessness to simply having serious accommodation difficulties, from having no fixed abode to living in a hostel or lodging house.

A problem with the concept of homelessness is the notion of a 'home'. A 'house' is generally taken to be synonymous with a dwelling or a physical structure, whereas a 'home' is not. A 'home' implies particular social relations, or activities within a physical structure, whereas a 'house' does not. The home as a social concept is strongly linked with a notion of family – the parental home, the marital home, the ancestral home. The word 'home' conjures up such images as personal warmth, comfort, stability and security, it carries a meaning beyond the simple notion of a shelter. It is interesting to consider the occasions when 'home' rather than 'house' is chosen as more appropriate to

8

a particular ideology. Looking at politicians' statements on owner-occupation, from both the Labour and Conservative parties, it becomes clear that the choice of word is not arbitrary. For example: 'for most people owning one's own home is a basic and natural desire' (DOE, 1977, p.50). On the other hand, the usual expression is to 'rent a house'. Again only a few researchers in the field of homelessness have recognized this breadth of meaning of the concept of home, and none has explicitly considered the implications of the emphasis on the family for individuals who do not belong to family households. Brandon (1973, p.8) criticized Shelter (the national campaigning organizaion for the homeless) for their emphasis on housing conditions and their neglect of emphasis on the home as a system of social relationships:

> Home or common habitation is seen as one of the common characteristics of the human family. When I go home – I am returning to a recognisable building with furniture, food and warmth, with my friends and family nearby. Being without a home conveys a sense of material as well as emotional deficit. Shelter . . . have regrettably used the term (homelessness) as synonymous with poor quality housing.

Furthermore, Shelter's concern with poor quality housing has been expressed in terms of its implications for the family, not for single people. Shelter defined as homeless 'in the true sense of the word' those people 'who live in conditions so bad that a civilised family life is impossible' (1972, p.9).

The housed-houseless question presents less of a problem – those with a roof over their heads versus those without might well serve as a workable definition, but 'homelessness' is the term which is generally employed. The problem arises over where the line can be drawn between those with 'homes' and those without. It is useful to consider the question in terms of a continuum with sleeping rough at one end and absolute security of tenure in the form of outright ownership at the other. There would be little disagreement with the notion of the former state as literally homeless and the latter as not. In between, however, lies an extensive grey area, ranging across hostels, hotels, temporary accommodation, sleeping on friends' floors, licences, to insecure private rented accommodation, mortgaged accommodation and so on.

There are two arguments developed here. The first is that homelessness is a socially determined and relative concept, that within the whole spectrum of different types of accommodation other factors come into play: the conditions and standard of the physical structure, its form and location, the form of the household and the relation to tenure of each member of the household, and the nature of actual and possible social relations within the physical structure and its environs. The second is that the definition of homelessness selected has major implications for the quantification and analysis of the causes of the problems, and also for policy and provision.

Social construction of homelessness

Homelessness is an historically and culturally specific concept. Like poverty (see Townsend, 1979, pp.50–3), it is a relative concept: people make judgments about their own level of deprivation on the basis of what they see around them. Thus, in a society where mud huts are the most prevalent forms of housing, and hence the norm, it is probable that their inhabitants would not, in isolation, consider themselves homeless. If, however, the mud hut dwellers were to compare themselves with those living in wealthier societies, or were themselves to live in a mud hut in one of those societies, the situation could be quite different. Subjectively, they might suddenly begin to see themselves as homeless, as Marx aptly expressed it (Marx quoted in Tucker, 1972, p.180):

> A house may be large or small; as long as the surrounding houses are equally small it satisfies all social demands for a dwelling. But let a palace arise beside the little house, and it shrinks from a little house to a hut . . . and however high it may shoot up in the course of civilization, if the neighbouring palace grows to an equal or even greater extent, the occupant of the relatively small house will feel more and more uncomfortable, dissatisfied and cramped within its four walls.

These mud hut inhabitants might also be considered homeless by others within the more affluent society. Recognized minimum standards in the construction of dwellings provide an interesting example of the way the ground has shifted. During different historical periods what is considered to be the right number and range of rooms and amenities and the optimum space standards are socially determined varying according to which social class the dwelling is intended for, the cost of building to these standards, the current economic climate, the strength of the working class, central and local government policies, the nature of the household and so on. Thus the decline of the improved standards implemented by the post-war Labour government which began in 1951 was later challenged by the Parker Morris Committee report[1] which 'pointed to the growth of real wages since the war, the increased stock of consumer durables owned by working-class families and the burgeoning interests at home by the individuals within the family' (Merrett, 1979, p.103). This report hence advocated increased space standards. What is relevant here is how far below recognized 'decent' standards does a dwelling have to fall before the household living there is considered to be without a proper home or homeless. In the Department of the Environment study (1981) of the single homeless, a squat was considered to be in this category. Was this decision made on the basis of the common physical poverty of squats, their insecurity or their usual short life? The answer is not given. A further relative point is contained in the Parker Morris report's concern: 'the important thing in the design of homes (is) to concentrate on satisfying the requirements of the families that are likely to live in them' (MHLG, 1961, p.4). This reflects the ideological primacy of the family household in relation to the 'home' discussed earlier.

Definitions of homelessness – the consequences

The range of definitions of homelessness is vast. Government research in its early days particularly, policy and legislation have defined homelessness in such a way as to circumscribe a narrow section of the population as homeless. From a statutory point of view definitions of homelessness have implications for delimiting a specific area of responsibility on the part of the local authority, and for quantification of the problem of homelessness.

On the former question the Housing (Homeless Persons) Act 1977 provides the best illustration of the process of delimitation of the homeless population, since the Act placed on local authority housing departments statutory responsibility for the housing of the homeless for the first time. Under the terms of the Act (S1–1, S2) a person is homeless if 'there is no accommodation, which *he*[2] and anyone who normally resides with *him* as a member of *his* family or anyone the housing authority consider is reasonable to reside with *him* is entitled to occupy', or if *he* has accommodation but cannot secure entry to it, or if it is probable that *his* occupation of it will lead to either, violence or real threats of violence from someone else residing there'[3] (my emphasis). However, not all households who are homeless according to this definition are eligible for housing. The Act defines categories of homeless people who are considered to be in 'priority need' for accommodation. The first and foremost category of 'priority need' household are those who have responsibility for dependent children. Single homeless people are only considered to be in priority need if they are 'vulnerable as a result of old age, mental illness and handicap, or physical disability or other special reasons'. (Housing (Homeless Persons) Act S.2(1)(c)). Thus, embodied at the heart of the Act is the centrality of the family to housing, and the notion that only 'special' groups of single people have as much right to housing.

The figures on households accepted by local authorities in London in 1981 as homeless under this Act support this argument: only 18 per cent of the total number of households accepted were single-person households despite the fact that single-person households accounted for approximately 40 per cent of all households in London (DOE, 1982, Table 7). However, the Act does not only proscribe the homeless through giving priority to specific forms of household, it also introduces the notion of 'intentional homelessness' i.e., if a local authority can prove that a household has become homeless 'intentionally', it is no longer under obligation to accept that household as 'homeless'. The term is clearly a discretionary one and has been used widely by some local authorities to blame households for their homelessness and to try to evade their responsibilities under the provisions of the Act. Thus, for example, households who become homeless through rent arrears, or through domestic violence are declared to be 'intentionally homeless' by some authorities. The Housing (Homeless Persons) Act therefore defines a concept of homelessness and then

12

delimits it to exclude certain categories of the homeless.

Nevertheless such definitions obviously serve a purpose. Priority need households and restrictive policies are necessary because local authorities cannot fulfil their responsibilities to all those who apply for housing as homeless. Hence the argument (see, for example, Pahl, 1980) that local authority housing departments adopt a gatekeeping role between the homeless and the limited stock of council houses.

The circumscription of homelessness relates directly to the quantification of the problem. The level of homelessness recorded by local authorities (and recorded by the Department of the Environment through the H1 returns) is the number of households accepted as homeless by the local authorities. All those households who are refused assistance or who fail to apply are excluded from the statistics. Thus, changes in the level of homelessness as revealed by Department of the Environment figures may simply reflect changes in local authority admittance policies. Research into homelessness which focuses on local authority provision for the homeless is similarly problematic. For example, the London County Council enquiry into London's homeless, which defined homeless people as those who come to the attention or into the care of any of the services of the Council by reason of homelessness (Greve, 1964, p.12) necessarily excluded from its statistics all those homeless people who were not eligible for welfare accommodation. As Greve pointed out (ibid., p.12), this meant that the investigation was effectively confined to young couples with children under sixteen who were provided shelter by the Welfare Department. Homeless couples without children, husbands of women admitted to the centres who were themselves excluded, single people, the elderly and parents of children who were wards of the State who could find nowhere to house their families, all failed to enter the record.

The problem of quantification raises again the question of where the line can be drawn between those with homes and those without. Obviously the further the line is drawn from the 'sleeping rough' end of the continuum, the larger the problem appears to be.

The implications for policy and provision are clear and not surprisingly therefore, politicians in government have tended to veer towards the narrowest definitions. For example, in 1969

David Ennals, then Minister of State for Health and Social Security, said (Shelter, 1969, p.9):

> I am speaking of truly homeless people – those who have
> come to welfare departments for shelter in temporary
> accommodation. There has been a great deal of exaggeration
> of the size of this problem and the numbers involved. I have
> even seen references to 'three million homeless'. This is
> really nonsense. In England and Wales there are 3,594
> families living in temporary accommodation.

Any estimation of the extent of homelessness which does not specify precisely what form of homelessness is being measured, be it those in temporary accommodation or those in poor housing conditions, is inevitably meaningless.

A similar problem in homelessness research arises in the evaluation of characteristics of the homeless population. Studies of the homeless which draw their sample from a particular point of provision, such as temporary accommodation, can only provide information about the specific group of homeless people using that accommodation. They will not necessarily tell us anything about the characteristics of the homeless people who are not eligible for, or who do not choose to go to, the institutional provision in question. This relates to the issue of whether concealed homelessness is similar to institutionalized homelessness: whether the homeless who are sleeping on friends' floors, living in insecure or tied accommodation, or adopting alternative housing solutions, are similar to the homeless who live in institutionalized provision for the homeless. There is no inherent logic for making this assumption. More realistic perhaps, is the assumption that there is a continuum of homelessness or housing need, along which individuals are located according to specific factors which warrant investigation. It is arguable, therefore, whether a study of the young single homeless in hostels (see for example, Diamond, 1975) can be generalized to describe the nature of young single homelessness at large. If it can, why do some young single homeless people end up in hostels, while others do not? These are questions which need to be considered.

Concealed homelessness has been largely ignored. The exception to the rule were several reports from voluntary organizations offering advice to the homeless (for example, Housing

Advice Switchboard, 1981) and the Department of Environment study (1981). Even those studies which have addressed the issue have failed to analyse the implications of adopting a broad and non-specific definition of homelessness. After Six (renamed Housing Advice Switchboard) defined homelessness as follows (1978, p.18):

> People are homeless if they do not have a fixed address –
> either they are literally homeless when they have nowhere
> to sleep that night, or they are in temporary accommodation,
> e.g. being put up by friends or in bed and breakfast. People
> are potentially homeless if they have to move or there is
> pressure on them to move.

Such a definition begs several questions. Does a long stay hostel which provides bed and breakfast constitute potential homelessness even if the household has resources to find alternative accommodation? Does hostility from another member of the household in a dwelling where there is inadequate space for all members of the household, constitute pressure to move? Who defines these terms – the housing adviser, the local authority housing department, the potentially homeless individual? There are no straightforward answers.

The Department of Environment study (1981) of the single homeless illuminates the serious problems which arise in attempting to construct a representative sample of all single homeless people, that is, both those in institutions for the homeless and those whose homelessness is concealed. Homelessness was defined in the research as (DOE, 1981, p.125):

1) being without adequate shelter now;
2) facing the loss of shelter within one month;
3) living in a situation of no security of tenure and being
   forced to seek alternative accommodation within a time
   period which the client considers to be immediate (for
   example, potential dischargees from institutions of all
   types; people living with friends and relatives in
   overcrowded conditions; or illegal tenancies);
4) those living in: reception centres, crash pads, derelict
   buildings, squats (unlicensed), hostels, lodging houses,
   cheap hotels and boarding houses.

15

Within such a broad range of categories of accommodation, how possible is it to draw the necessary line? For example, how is 'adequate shelter' to be assessed? The researchers' answer was that the 'client's view was taken as far as possible' (ibid., p.126), but adequate for what? Is a drummer living in accommodation where she/he cannot play drums, living in inadequate shelter?

Equally serious a question is how can a representative sample of all these different homeless groups be drawn? What proportion of the homeless sample should be those living in insecure accommodation and what proportion those living in hostels? The problem would not arise if the different homeless groups were not aggregated, or if it could be shown that there were no significant differences between the groups on the characteristics or variables that were to be explored. If, however, the different groups are aggregated without analysing the differences between groups and conclusions drawn, the results are liable to be meaningless. In the Department of Environment survey, 521 individuals were drawn from the categories of provision listed above in seven areas in England, and aggregated on some variables in precisely this way. Although attempts were made to select a representative sample of the single homeless, the selection was inevitably arbitrary. If only certain categories of provision existed in a specific area, these were the only places to be sampled. Thus, for example, in Tower Hamlets the sample was drawn exclusively from a large hostel and night shelters, whereas in Haringey the sample was drawn from a small hostel, YMCAs, and advice centres. Differences between the homeless in the two areas could therefore be attributed to differences in provision rather than differences in the homeless population.

One example from the report will serve to illustrate the problem of aggregating data collected from a range of homeless groups. One conclusion was that a major difference between men and women was that homeless women were much more likely than men to have office jobs (ibid., p.27). This finding can be entirely explained by the sampling procedure. In terms of institutionalized provision for the homeless there is far more provision for women in up-market hostels which cater for white collar workers than there is emergency provision for the homeless in direct access hostels where employment is not a criterion for acceptance (Austerberry and Watson, 1983, p.16). The picture is reversed for men. More women in the sample were drawn from these up-market hostels than men, hence the conclusion. Likewise in Haringey, where the highest proportion of women were found *and* the highest proportion of office workers, it is no surprise to see that over half the sample were drawn from up-market and small hostels.

Concepts of homelessness

Concepts of homelessness have changed over the years as the following two chapters show. In the same way as definitions of homelessness have implications for research and policy, so also does its conceptualization. There are two poles to the wide spectrum of attitudes. At one end, researchers locate homelessness within an analysis of the overall housing system (Greve, 1964, p.16):

> Any report on the causes of homelessness would be incomplete without taking the wider social and economic environment in consideration. The relentless high demand for housing in London, rising rents and house prices, and homelessness are all part (and products) of the intricate web of economic and social changes.

At the other end the emphasis is on psychological factors. The blame for homelessness lies with the individual: 'To his environment, the down and out contributes nothing. To exist in it he must be as psychopathic as his neighbour' (Whiteley, 1955). In the same vein in his study of 'Skid Row', Bahr (1973, p.17), draws our attention to Caplow's definition: 'Homelessness is a condition of detachment from society characterised by the absence or attenuation of the affiliative bonds that link settled persons to a network of interconnected social structures.'

The psychopathological approach has a long history in attitudes to the homeless, for example (Gray, 1931, p.358): 'A very large population of boys upon the road are mentally "peculiar", indeed if they were not they would not be on the road.'

So, too, does the wider economic and social approach as the historical analysis of homelessness shows. Clearly, a psychological emphasis implies the need for institutional provision for the homeless where some form of psychiatric treatment or social

17

work is provided. The economic and social approach sees homelessness as deriving primarily from a lack of housing: the solution, therefore, is posed in terms of the need for more accommodation above all else. Our sympathies lie with the latter approach.

The specificity of women's position in the home and of their homelessness

A further interesting dimension of the ambiguous nature of homelessness is the relativity of its meaning both between different forms of households and within the household unit itself. We have already referred to the dominant family model in relation to definitions of homelessness at a statutory and non-statutory level. There are several reasons for this, not least the centrality of the family to housing policy and provision and the marginalization of single people which is explored more fully in a later chapter. An important aspect, however, is the visibility of homelessness. The homelessness of families with children tends to be very exposed. If a family has nowhere to live the situation is evident. For the majority of families, because dependent children are involved and because of their size, there is frequently no possibility of staying with friends or relatives since most people do not have much extra space available. Thus the majority of families without a place to live will present themselves as homeless to the local housing department. Single people's homelessness, on the other hand, can be more easily concealed. It is easier for a single person to stay with friends or relatives or to find employment with accommodation tied to it, than it is for a family.

The second point is that the sexual division of labour within the household has implications for different household members' relation to the 'home' and hence to 'homelessness'. Once the relativity of the concept of homelessness is recognized, and the structural position of household members in relation to the home is taken into account, one individual (in a household) may be potentially homeless according to a broad definition of the term, while another is not. This has specific implications for women because of their primary role within the family as housewife and mother. Despite the removal of some domestic tasks from the

18

home (through the advent in the public sector of schools and social and health services, and through the growth of laundries and pre-cooked and processed foods, for example) women continue to take the major responsibility for domestic work and childcare. Only 27 per cent of women whose youngest child is between nought and four years are employed in full- or part-time work (DE and OPCS, 1983, Table 5). A 1965 survey (OPCS, 1968) found 27 per cent of working housewives received no assistance with domestic duties, with 45 per cent of those who had some help, having help with the washing-up and under 25 per cent reporting help with time-consuming tasks such as 'cooking and preparing meals' and 'washing, ironing and mending'. This division of labour within the household has been the subject of much feminist analysis, and is commonly referred to as the domestic labour debate (see, for example, Himmelweit and Mohun, 1977). It is not our intention to explore this debate here, the essential theme of our argument being that women's domestic role has implications for their relation to the 'home' and the housing market generally.

Further, women's centrality to the home is not straightforward. There is a prevalent assumption which derives from the patriarchal nature of the family that the man is the head of the household: 'the man's home is his castle'. Even when a woman is working, this notion often still holds, despite the contradictions it may entail. For example, the *Interviewers' Manual of Social and Community Planning Research* (1977, p.54), which defines the head of household as the man who owns or rents the property, or is in tied accommodation because of his job, states: 'there is only one exception: if a wife owns the property or has her name on the rent book or has the property because of her job, her husband is regarded as head of household provided that he is resident'. The expectation that the male head of household is the chief breadwinner, and that a woman will be supported financially by her husband, has profound consequences for her access to housing. A major part of a man's support of his family will be the roof over its head (consider the old custom of the bridegroom carrying the bride over the threshold) be it in the form of rent or mortgage repayments. This payment often amounts to a considerable sum (an average of 14 per cent of gross male earnings (Family Expenditure Survey 1981)) and tends to increase proportionately amongst lower income groups. Thus housing costs represent a crucial part of the disposal of men's wages. This sexual division is further reinforced, as feminists have argued (Cambell and Charlton, 1978) by workers' and trade unionists' demand for a 'family wage' – a wage adequate to support a man and family. Until recently it was indeed common practice for the man to be favoured as tenant or mortgagor, thus reinforcing women's subordinate position once again. Although this practice is changing, (with local authorities and buildings societies tending to grant more joint tenancies and mortgages[4]) where, as is often the case, the man is the primary wage earner in the family and controls the finances, the position of the woman is still dependent.

In examining women's domestic role and economic dependence within the family, it becomes clear that according to a relative definition of homelessness (where factors such as the conditions, form and location of the physical structure, and the relation to tenure, are considered) women are likely to be located at a different point on the home-to-homelessness continuum than their male partners. If the physical conditions of the house are poor the woman, as domestic labourer, is usually the member of the household to be most affected. Cramped kitchens, dampness, thin walls, and broken lifts in high rise dwellings, for example, make taking care of the home and rearing young children even more difficult and time consuming. Similarly, the design attributes of the dwelling and its spatial relation to the urban and social environment have a specific relevance to women. High rise flats with no communal facilities or playschemes for children, exacerbate women's isolation in the home. Maisonettes built around a central area, old terraces, and well-planned estates better serve women's needs in their domestic role. The distance of a dwelling from the local school, hospital, community centre, shopping centre, and the efficiency of the local transport system, affect women specifically in their role as housewife and mother. Lack of employment opportunities locally may further reinforce women's domestic role.

Second, within the household the ultimate control of a tenancy, mortgage or property owned outright lies with the person who holds the tenure, subject of course, to any statutory consideration. It is the tenant who can withold rent or is responsible for rent arrears which accrue, and the owner (or mortgagor) who has the benefit or difficulties associated with owning a capital asset. Where the male householder is the sole or major wage earner and controls the family's income, the woman can find herself dependent on her partner for her housing security. If, for example, he spends all the rent/mortgage, and the household is threatened with eviction, there is little that a woman in such a position can do.

Finally, the privatized and individualized way housing is consumed reflects and reinforces dominant social relations within the house or home. The sanctity and privacy of marriage have been enshrined in legislation, and in the attitudes and policy of social agencies. Domestic violence and rape within marriage have traditionally escaped social intervention; what a husband does with his 'own' wife in his 'own' home is his business. Thus, the house may be a place of violence and imprisonment, where a woman fears for her safety. On the other hand, it is a domain which a man in such a situation can control and define.

Within what may appear to be a cohesive family household, relation to tenure, physical and locational attributes, and/or internal social relations can thus transform the dwelling into a 'home' for one member of the household, while for another the dwelling may be little more than a physical structure. Such a person, we would argue, is potentially homeless. It is clear, therefore, that exploring the relativity of the concept of homelessness makes the possibility of constructing a definition of the concept increasingly elusive. Women's domestic role, their lack of financial independence, and the lack of housing provision for single women, makes the notion of concealed homelessness particularly significant for women.

The selection of the sample of homeless women

One of our objectives was to explore the nature of female homelessness. Recognizing at an early stage the difficulty of constructing a definition of homelessness, we worked in terms of a notion of a home-to-homelessness continuum. A coherent ordering of the hierarchy of accommodation on this continuum seemed to be the following: sleeping rough, emergency direct-access hostel or refuge accommodation, restricted-access hostel accommodation, and finally a conglomerate of non-institutionalized and hidden unsatisfactory and insecure forms of accommodation. This included staying with friends or relatives in overcrowded conditions, tied or private rented accommodation where the woman is forced to leave or is under pressure to leave, or where the conditions were very poor, and accommodation in which the woman was forced to leave due to domestic dispute or violence.

The female sleeping rough population were excluded – first because only a minority of 'homeless' women sleep rough for an extended period, and second because many of the women who sleep rough also use hostels.[5] Selecting a sample from the institutionalized emergency forms of provision for homeless women presented few problems, Direct-access hostels and women's aid centres for battered women tend to be seen by social workers and housing departments, and by the majority (but not all) of the residents, as accommodation for the homeless. Residents frequently share rooms and the accommodation is far from the normative concept of a home. Furthermore, the majority of research into the homeless has focused on this form of provision. However, finding women to interview in the more up-market hostels where residents tend to have their own rooms and stay for longer periods of time proved more difficult. Since there are more places available for women in these hostels than in direct access hostels such a sample seemed vital. Despite our view that these hostels were located at the homeless end of the 'home-homeless' continuum, many of the managers of this provision did not agree. Instead, we were told that the women in their hostels were not homeless and that the study was of no relevance to them. In the four up-market hostels where we gained access the women were a self-selecting group; they were the ones who considered themselves homeless at some level. In the end we interviewed fewer (twenty-one) women from these hostels than from the direct-access hostels (seventy) and women's aid centres (eleven) simply because of problems of access.

The difficulties of defining 'concealed homelessness' have been discussed. Equally difficult is finding a sample of this group if homelessness is not visible. Women's homelessness, according to a broad definition of the term, is largely concealed due to the lack of available and affordable provision. This argument is substantiated by data on single individuals approaching a housing advice agency for homeless single people: in 1981 the ratio of female to male homeless single enquirers was 4:1 (Austerberry, Schott and Watson, 1984). We wanted to explore the 'home-to-homelessness' continuum and to expand the concept of homelessness beyond institutionalized homelessness, as well as to investigate the similarities and differences between institutionalized and concealed homeless women. We thus adopted a broad definition of the concealed homeless similar to Norris' definition (1974, p.7): ' "Homeless" was to include any state where present accommodation was inadequate for reasons which seemed good to the applicant.'

The women were contacted through an advice agency for the single homeless in London. Despite the difficulty of tracing such a sample, sixty concealed homeless women were finally interviewed. All the women were over the age of twenty-five. First, because there is already a body of research into the young single homeless. Second, the problem of young single homelessness appears to be a substantially different one, one reason being that the majority (90 per cent) of young single people eventually marry. We were interested, therefore, in looking at the status of 'single' for women across a wide age range, and its implications for women's lack of access to any secure permanent accommodation.

Although the interviews took place in London and thus shed greatest light on the housing experiences of women in that city, they illuminate issues that are of more general concern (not least because many of the past experiences of the women occurred outside of London). The interaction of women's family and labour market positions to effectively marginalize them in the housing market, the structuring of housing to excude single people and in particular single women, and the meaning of homelessness for women derives from their primary domestic role; these are issues not merely specific to London. Nevertheless, the articulation of patriarchal and capitalist social relations and the structure of housing and labour markets take very different spatial forms. In the terms of this study, the outcome of losing accommodation for a woman in a city where there is a large public rental sector and high unemployment such as Glasgow, will differ from the outcome in an outer London

23

borough like Sutton where the public sector is small and registered unemployment figures are lower. Likewise, gender relations in London, where a large proportion of households are single, and women can thus experience a certain degree of autonomy, differ from gender relations in an area where the nuclear family is the most prevalent social unit and women's labour force participation is low. The specific housing, employment and social histories of the women interviewed thus have to be seen in the context of London where the private rented sector is small and expensive, where house prices are high, where there is more hostel provision for women than in other regions, where local authority policies range widely between inner and outer London areas and where the proportion of women in the workforce is relatively high. Nevertheless, these housing, employment and family histories also throw light on important underlying relations and structures which imply some similarity of experience across time and space.

The four sample groups were chosen to represent four kinds of housing circumstances which were responses to homelessness. We aimed to explore the similarities and differences between women who are located at various points towards the homeless end of the home-homelessness continuum, and also to explore the similarities and differences between these women and the average female population. By selecting different groups of homeless women and comparing them, we hoped to show the problems associated with treating homeless women as a homogenous group, and to clarify the social and economic processes which structure homeless women's positions on the edge of the housing market. However, before examining the experiences of the homeless women who were interviewed and their definitions of homelessness, we analyse female homelessness historically in order to understand the nature of female homelessness provision and concepts of female homelessness today. This is the focus of the following two chapters. The final chapter in the first part of this book addresses the centrality of the family household to housing policy and provision, and shows how single women's homelessness is intricately related to the marginality of single-person housing provision and the sexual division of labour.

Chapter 3

Homeless women – an historical perspective: from industrialization to the Second World War

An historical analysis of women's housing and homelessness is interesting because it reveals that many of the current ideologies and attitudes towards the homeless originate in earlier periods. Questions asked in the late nineteenth and early twentieth centuries are still being addressed, and many of the problems appear to be similar. Thus, issues such as the conflict between 'woman as worker' and 'woman as homemaker', the significance of matrimonial property rights, and the social reformers' concern with female sexuality and its protection, all of which were apparent in the Victorian period, continue to be of relevance today. Likewise, early studies of housing poverty and homelessness (Rowntree, 1902), and literary descriptions of down and out life (Orwell, 1933) have their present day counterparts (Townsend, 1979; Sandford, 1971). Many of the charitable, voluntary and statutory agencies concerned with the issue have their roots in this early period, and an investigation into their origins and early practices provides illuminating insights into their present attitudes and methods of functioning.

The focus here is on the late nineteenth century and the genesis of social reform, although we also look briefly at the inter-war period. The following chapter examines the post-war period. The homelessness discussed in these chapters is inevitably homelessness as it was defined at the specific time. It is, doubtless, possible to get beyond this level of analysis but it would require different forms of historical investigation such as verbal histories which we had neither time nor resources to pursue.

The Industrial Revolution and the Victorian era

Homelessness is not a new phenomenon. Every society has had its wanderers, vagrants, beggars and missionaries, many of whom had no place to call their home. However, stigma was not necessarily attached to this mobility, since many of the lay and clerical wanderers, such as peddlars, herbalists and musicians, clearly depended on moving for their livelihood (Ribton-Turner, 1887).

It is not until the Industrial Revolution and the increased urbanization of the early Victorian period that homelessness becomes defined as a serious social problem. The needs of industry for large concentrations of labour in the urban centres were met by thousands of men and women, young and old, flocking to the cities to seek employment in the factories, mills and shops. Through several decades urban settlements expanded at a steady rate. Where did all these new immigrants to the cities find accommodation? There were several possibilities and, not surprisingly, the housing option available related primarily to the economic status of the person concerned. Before looking at the major forms of housing provision which developed as a response to the massive increased demand for housing by single people throughout the nineteenth century, and women's homelessness which resulted from lack of provision, we need to understand women's social and economic position in Victorian society.

The dominance of the family to the rhetoric of Victorian life, that is, the life of the middle and upper classes, is well known (Beales, 1949, p.344): 'Every Englishman's home was his castle. In its sanctities and privacy a man might escape from the trials of the outer world and be safe from its prying eyes.'

The home represented security and comfort, the woman within it was the Perfect Lady, the idealized feminine wife/mother, the homemaker, the pure and womanly woman (Wilson, 1977, p.22). Even the Census extolled the domestic sphere (Census, 1851, p.64): '. . . it requires no argument to prove that the wife, the mother, the mistress of an English family fills offices and discharges duties of no ordinary importance . . . The most important production of a country is its population.'

To the middle/upper classes, therefore, the preservation of the

26

family and decent morals were of prime importance and needed to be upheld. They were fearful of the breakdown of family life and sexual promiscuity that poor and overcrowded housing conditions and increased urbanization seemed to imply. Nevertheless, various factors militated against this domestic ideal, not least the fact, first of all, that this ideal was predominantly a middle-class, not a working-class one. Second was the general recognition that women were becoming increasingly active in the paid workforce.[1] Third there was a surplus of women within the population. Finally, the massive shortage of decent accommodation available for poorer families made the domestic ideal unrealisable at a material level.

In comparison with men's wages during the nineteenth century women's wages were very low. Mill (1849; Bk2,Ch.14) raises the issue in his *Principles of Political Economy*: 'It deserves consideration why the wages of women are generally lower, and very much lower, than those of men, the minimum (wage) in their case is the pittance absolutely requisite for the sustenance of one human being.'

Mill suggested that the occupations accessible to women, due to 'law and custom', were comparatively so few that the field of their possible employment was overcrowded. This inevitably led to greater competition for jobs, and the ability on the employers' part to keep wages low. Women's low wages in this period of industrialization clearly must have restricted their ability to pay for accommodation.

Married women's property rights also had a significant impact on women's autonomy, or rather, lack of autonomy. Under common law, married women had no separate identity from their husbands 'As the saying went, in law "husband and wife are one person, and the husband is that person" '. (Holcombe, 1977, p.4) This amounted to a husband assuming full legal possession and control over all his wife's property, with slightly greater control over her personal 'chattels' and leasehold land, than over her freehold land. A man could thus use and dispose of his wife's personal property and make a will disposing of his wife's personal property as well as his own property, including that which had come to him from his wife, as he wished. If he died intestate his widow never received more than half of the property. In contrast, a wife could only bequeath her personal property with her husband's consent, and if she died intestate all her property remained her husband's. The only recourse to the common-law rules and practices were the principles and practices of equity which recognized a wife's existence and right to property as separate from her husband. By applying to the courts of equity which proceeded on the basis that although an individual could not hold property, it could be held for his/her benefit by a trustee, a married woman could acquire the same rights over her property as an unmarried woman. This meant that she could receive income from it, sell it or give it away, and leave it to anyone she wished. However, the only women who were legally protected were those of the wealthier classes, since proceedings in the equity courts were expensive. It was estimated that only one woman in ten had separate property in equity (ibid., p.8). Thus the majority of married women were effectively propertyless and therefore totally financially dependent upon their husbands. This meant that a woman wanting to separate from her husband and find separate housing, would have had tremendous difficulties within such a system.

Housing provision for single women prior to 1880

Until the final two decades of the nineteenth century, when social reformers began to perceive a housing crisis, and hence to intervene in the market, there were four major forms of housing provision available to single women in housing need. These were lodging or boarding with a household, lodging houses, tied accommodation, and the casual ward. The distinction between lodging within a household and a lodging house is not a clear one. The Housing Report of the 1831 Census laid down their definitional guidelines as follows:

> In the case of business establishments and boarding houses, where any doubt has arisen in regard to the nature of the occupation, the residents have been included in the private family class when the number of business assistants or boarders was not greater than the number of members of the employers' or householder's family (including domestic servants).

The other convention adopted in the Censuses during this period was that boarders (who ate with the family) were part of the family of the occupier, but lodgers were to be counted as single families. Taking in lodgers was an important form of livelihood for widows and women without support, with as many as 80 per cent of 'lodging house keepers' being women (Davidoff, 1979, p.86). It was customary for landladies and landlords to advertise for lodgers in the newspapers, specifying the kind of person wanted, frequently emphasizing respectability as an important attribute. 'Gentlewomen' are frequently mentioned in advertisements for board and lodging in newspapers such as the *Womans Gazette*.

The Victorian middle classes, however, considered living in lodgings to be unrespectable and shameful, both for those letting out lodgings and the lodgers themselves (ibid., p.68). Lodgings represented a lack of privacy, so important to the preservation of the family, and a casualness of social relationships and mixing of social groups. The connection between the home and the patriarchal family is firmly established in the introduction to the 1851 Census: 'The possession of an entire house is strongly desired by every Englishman: for it throws a sharp well-defined circle around his family and hearth – the shrine of his sorrows, joys and meditations.'

Not surprisingly the notion of lodgings for women was considered a serious matter for concern: 'any arrangement which, by supplying cheap accommodation encourages young women to leave the shelter, however poor, of their own home and offers them an opportunity of living without any restrictions or oversight . . . exercises a decidedly harmful influence' (Mrs B. Booth, quoted in Davidoff, 1979, p.74)

Not only is the distinction between lodgings and lodging houses a problematic one, so too is the distinction between different kinds of lodging houses. As Booth (1898, p.206) wrote:

> The provision to be found in the metropolis for those who are homeless – or perhaps it would be more accurate to say, those who enjoy no family life[2] – has a wide range. From the luxury of the West End residential club to the 'fourpenny doss' of Bangor Street is but a degree.

It is clear from reports at the time that some lodging house keepers were concerned to maintain high standards in their establishments. A 'Superintendent' of a larger lodging house wrote (Children's Employment Commission, 1864, p.119):

> We have more than 30 young women resident here; most of them are between the ages of 18 and 30. . . . Nearly 2/3 are dressmakers; some few are milliners. . . . We require two references with each girl and are obliged always to keep a very strict watch over them all. I have unfortunately had to dismiss two or three; they were receiving notes from gentlemen, and making appointments to meet them. It might all be innocent, but for the sake of the rest, we were obliged to send them away. . . . Many are very respectable quiet girls.

At the other end of the scale large numbers of men and women were crowded together in appalling conditions. For the thousands of people flocking to the cities for employment with little or no income, the common lodging house was the most notable source of housing. Landlords bought dwellings, often in a poor state of disrepair and rented the rooms out to as many people as they could feasibly squeeze in. Such housing became an attractive source of investment for those such as artisans and shopkeepers with a little capital looking for speedy profit. Again, the emphasis of Victorian morality was concern about the lack of control over women's sexuality, it was women who were constantly mentioned in discussions of these 'dens of vice' (Mayhew, 1851, quoted in Quennell, ed., 1949):

> The indiscriminate admixture of the sexes among adults, in many of these places, is another evil. Even in some houses considered of the better sort, men and women, husbands and wives, old and young, strangers and acquaintances, sleep in the same apartment and if they choose, in the same bed. Any remonstrance at some act of gross depravity, or impropriety on the part of women not so utterly hardened as the others, is met with abuse and derision.

Nevertheless, many women had little choice but to sleep in these lodging houses; one estimate of numbers thus accommodated by the 1850s in England and Wales being 80,000. Interestingly, some writers commented on a notable difference between the female and male residents: the women tended to be more concerned about their domestic environment (Higgs, 1910, p.159): 'The woman is instinctively inclined to make the place a home, but the man more often uses it simply as a place wherein to sleep. . . . These women are in the kitchen almost the whole day.'

This theme re-emerges as a central issue in our own interviews with homeless women.

Tied accommodation was another source of housing for women. In a survey of the 1851 Census Davidoff (1979, p.79) found that male lodgers outnumbered female lodgers by between two or three to one. This disparity, she argues, can be explained by the importance of domestic service as a form of female employment which also provided bed and board. The 1851 Census (p.65) details the massive extent of this form of employment: of the 1,038,791 domestic servants enumerated, 905,165 were female. Equally important was the growth of employment for women in the drapery and allied trades. In many shops and dressmaking workshops, in particular those attached to the large silk drapers and (proto) department stores, 'living-in' was a condition of employment. Of the 2,420,173 people whose occupation was 'concerned with the dress of both sexes', 1,787,460 were women (ibid). Most of these women would have lived at the workplace. Thus, tied accommodation was clearly a significant feature of female employment in the nineteenth century.

Finally, for those with absolutely no other option, there were the casual wards. The casual wards were administered under the Poor Law Acts which imposed a legal responsibility on localities to provide food and shelter for all who were utterly destitute. In line with the ideology prevalent in the 1820s, that beggars could make more money from begging than from a hard day's work, the Poor Law Amendment Act of 1834 enshrined the notion that a person receiving relief should always be worse off than the lowest paid worker. The workhouse, therefore, became the place for those who were prepared to give up freedom for food and shelter under extremely repressive conditions. The casual ward was established as part of the poor law institution to provide shelter for those who were supposedly temporarily out of work and seeking employment. However, the system made the search for employment virtually impossible. Anyone taken into the casual ward for the night was obliged to stay for two nights and one day during which they were subjected to a rigorously strict system. For supper they were given a pint mug of gruel or porridge before being locked in cells until the following day. They were then given the task of oakum-picking and stone breaking, the women either doing the same task as men, although half the amount, or domestic work. If they did not finish their oakum picking by 7 o'clock they had to stay up until they did. Instead of encouraging people to seek employment after a night's bed this system acted as a form of detention. One woman applying elsewhere for a bed said (Higgs, 1910, p.175):

> Can't you take me in. I'm dead beat and if I walk about tonight, I can't go to work in the morning. . . . I can't go to the 'casual' or I'll lose it (the job), they won't let you out till it's too late for work.

The deliberate policy of making the casual ward as unpleasant as possible, and making it as difficult as possible for someone to find work the following day was no doubt intended to minimize the number of people in the wards, a policy which appears to have been successful. Women constituted a sizeable proportion of those using the casual wards, the ratio being 79 per cent men and 21 per cent women in 1886, (Ribton-Turner, 1887, p.325). However, why there were actually less women than men is a matter for conjecture. One reason possibly was that homeless women would be more inclined to stay in a common lodging house, since a 'casual' was compelled to move on after two nights to another ward, often a considerable distance away. Second, women tended not to be part of the mobile labour force to the same extent as men, and third, the conditions in the workhouse probably proved unacceptable to many women.

Moral and physical welfare – the upsurge of social and government concern

Hand in hand with the discussion of single women's inadequate housing and ill-paid employment during this period, a concern about the growing numbers of women working as prostitutes is expressed. There were several connections between housing and prostitution. Overcrowded living conditions were perceived by the middle classes to pose a threat to decent moral living and family life and specifically a threat to the ideal of the pure untainted Victorian woman. This threat acted as a spur to intervention by both the State and social reformers. Also, numerous women testified in court that they were remaining in brothels because they could not find any alternative accommodation (Walkowitz, 1977, p.84). Related to this was the reluctance by landladies to let rooms to prostitutes for fear of losing public respectability or being harrassed by the police (ibid., p.88). Of course it was not the case as some suggested, that prostitution was simply a result of poor housing. As the more radical thinkers recognized, prostitution for many women was the only way of earning an income, or of supplementing the low wages their employment offered. One sympathizer wrote (Higgs, 1910, p.16):

> Large and, we fear, increasing numbers of women and girls
> are driven into professional prostitution by the fruitless
> endeavour to find respectable employment. That this
> number is further increased by those who are ill-housed,
> especially when in search of employment, succumbing to the
> evil conditions which surround them, will hardly be doubted.

Thus there was a range of opinion on the issue: some blamed bad housing, while others emphasized economic considerations. Interesting, however, is the recognition of the material base of prostitution, and a desire to come up with material solutions. This concern about the moral welfare of the population, particularly the female population, was compounded by fears of physical ill-health among the new labour force of the cities. Various groups and individuals thus saw fit to intervene to remedy the situation. The State represented one major form of intervention, and the social reformers, who themselves fell into a number of groups, the other.

Victorian middle-class distaste with shared living arrangements prompted one of the earliest Victorian pieces of punitive and interventionist legislation: the Common Lodging Houses Acts of 1851 and 1853 which were proposed and drafted by Lord Shaftesbury. Under these Acts local authorities were required to register and regularly inspect the common lodging houses and enforce minimum standards of sanitation, and to remove sick people to hospital. They were set up to reach 'to the homes and health of the people benevolently intruding on their habits' (Parliamentary Papers, 1852–3, p.528). However, the Acts had little effect, one of the difficulties being the problem of defining what constituted a common lodging house. Despite the fact that there were penalties to landlords who did not comply, common lodging houses remained overcrowded and often filthy throughout the nineteenth century.

In order to proscribe prostitution, which was seen as a major symptom of poor living conditions and lack of housing, the Contagious Diseases Acts of 1864, 1866 and 1869 were passed. This legislation forced prostitutes, or women suspected of being prostitutes to register with the police and to undergo compulsory medical examination. Once again women were thus elected to bear the brunt of Victorian morality. The Acts had several effects. One was an increase in the social isolation of prostitutes, and a shift in the prostitutes' self-perception, as a result of the public exposure to which they were subjected through police registration and examination procedures (Walkowitz, 1977, p.81). Another problem was that through police harassment and surveillance, once a woman was registered as a prostitute it was virtually impossible to have her name removed unless she left the area or married. Not surprisingly, therefore, the Acts met with a lot of resistance and public demonstrations were organized in their defence.

The reports from local government conferences held on poor relief and the treatment of the 'casual poor' during this period confirm this punitive approach, and again the treatment of women is singled out for attention. For example, the conference of 1872 made the following resolutions specifically affecting women: that outdoor relief (that is, outside of the workhouse) should not be granted to any woman alleging herself to be deserted by her husband, except on satisfactory proof of such desertion, nor, except in special cases, to any able-bodied widow without children, or with one child only, after the first six months of her widowhood. (Local Government Board, 1872–3). Overall, the report does not reflect a caring concern for the fate of those in hardship, rather, a condemnatory tone rings through. It is interesting to see that the clause requiring proof of desertion is echoed 100 years later in the Housing (Homeless Persons) Act 1977 clause which requires proof of 'unintentional homelessness' on the part of the homeless person.

The huge upsurge of activity among social reformers in the last three decades of the nineteenth century and the early twentieth century encompassed individuals and organizations of extremely varied persuasion and motivation. Attitudes to, and activities around, housing and homelessness sharply illuminate these differences in emphasis. The focus here is on the approach of those active in the field from the early 1870s until the First World War. Despite some overlap the groups can be loosely characterized as follows: religious bodies, social reformers of the Charity Organization Society, sanitary reformers, employers and providers of accommodation for working girls, and radicals.

An important new development was the work of the Salvation Army and the Church Army. The Salvation Army, inaugurated in 1878, was the more numerically significant of the two. In 1890 General Booth's *Darkest England and the Way Out* (so called, in comparison to Darkest Africa) was first published. This rhetorical tract explored the problem of destitution amongst men and women in great depth, the theories expounded there being an important influence on Salvation Army thinking in subsequent years. In some respects his approach was more sympathetic and less punitive than other interventions in the area at the time. He emphasized both the moral and the material, that is, that a 'man' must not only change 'his character and conduct which constitute the reasons for his failure in the battle of life' but also that 'the remedy, to be effectual, must change the circumstances of the individual when they are the cause of his wretched condition and lie beyond his control' (Booth, 1890, pp.85–6). Again, women play a central part in his doctrine, but Booth's attitude was less blame-oriented than many other social reformers of his time. Women had special needs which must be met and, prostitutes were victims who, once they had (ibid., p.13):

'consented to buy their right to earn their living by the sacrifice of their virtue, then they are treated as a slave and an outcast by the very men who have ruined them.'

As a response the Salvation Army engaged in the provision of rescue homes for young women who had been prostitutes. By 1890 there were thirteen homes accommodating 307 women. The aim of these was to reform the women and show them the 'highway of truth, virtue and religion', restore them to their friends and relatives or train them for domestic service – widely considered at the time to be a form of safe employment and housing. Booth's vision also included a plan for preventive homes for young women who had not yet 'fallen' but were in danger of doing so – again reflecting a somewhat sympathetic recognition of the limited choices for a young unemployed woman. Similar homes were established by other individuals and bodies throughout this period, with varying emphasis on reform and shelter.

To tackle homelessness more generally the Salvation Army opened its first food and shelter depot for men in Limehouse in 1888, and in 1891 the first women's shelter capable of accommodating forty women in Cardiff. Booth in his great 'scheme' for the future proposed to increase their number, and by 1900 Salvation Army provision reached 14,000 beds for men and women. The standards in many of these institutions were spartan, the premises often being converted from former factories (Brandon, n.d., p.2) and inevitably the religious input was not lacking, 'rousing Salvation meetings' being held in the evenings. These were not compulsory, but 'residents wanted to come and many found friends, counsel and salvation' there (Booth, 1970, p.99). According to one historian (Sandall, 1955, p.107) the local authorities did not initially welcome the shelters, in fact the officers had to overcome determined opposition. The Church Army also intervened in this area although it operated on a much smaller scale. Its emphasis, unlike the Salvation Army, was on smaller units and self-help.

Aside from religious institutions an abundance of night refuges run by voluntary organizations were established during the second half of the nineteenth century and it was to these that the Charity Organization Society directed its attention in 1870. The Charity Organization Society was founded in 1869 with an idea of charity which claimed to reconcile the divisions in society, to remove poverty and to produce a happy, self-reliant community. The organization of charity was an attempt to co-ordinate the work of charitable bodies, but it quickly became a wider movement to reform society. The emphasis was placed on the individual, the need to restore a person's self-respect and spirit and to get them to stand on their own feet – to fight their weakness of character. Simply to give material relief just because someone needed it was deemed to do more harm than good. This attitude was reflected in Sir Charles Trevelyan's speech at the 1870 conference (Mowat, 1961, p.51):

> The London predatory class pass from casual wards to night refuges, and from one night refuge to another; and the existence of this great proletaire class was in great degree owing to these institutions. These people are in a far better position than persons in the highest ranks of society.

Illustrated here is the recurring theme expressed by the reformers that not only does charitable provision create the problem it has set out to solve, but also that people receiving charity actually do very well for themselves. Thus, night refuges were urged to take on a remedial character, and to vet vagrants on arrival, not simply admitting all and sundry. According to the Society, many of the refuges adopted their principles.

The Charity Organization Society was also specifically involved with homeless people in 1894 when it submitted a report on the 'Homeless Poor of London', to a committee established to investigate the subject. The report recommended that some of the large night refuges be converted into small homes for the 'treatment' of the homeless (that is, helping them to find 'better ways of living'). It is interesting to note that this idea found currency at such an early date, for this was an important theme in the 1970s.

Linked to the Charity Organization Society as one of its district organizers was Octavia Hill who founded the first model lodging house in 1864 with financial support from Ruskin. Her belief was that the poor needed tuition and guidance in their lives, and that by lifting people out of despair and insisting on their self-improvement, they would start to lead cleaner and better lives and pay their rent more regularly. Octavia Hill's influence was considerable, giving rise to a substantial number of philanthropic housing associations, which adopted her principles and practices, throughout London. However, although the women of the families tended to bear the brunt of her methods, the focus of her work was with poor families, not the single homeless. Moreover, philanthropic housing for families usually enforced rules against lodgers.

37

Octavia Hill's work began at a time when many Victorians saw the destitute classes as a threat to moral and social stability. Some reformers emphasized sanitary reform as the key to the problem, a view shared in part by Octavia Hill. Chadwick's early campaign for sanitary reform had evolved by the second half of the century into a broader movement for sanitary and moral reform. Overcrowding and ill-health were not the only important issues, sexual promiscuity, degeneracy and mob violence were seen to be equally worrying threats. Nevertheless, as Gauldie (1974, p.139) points out: 'the philosophy of public health dominated all nineteenth century thinking about social reform', and much of the housing legislation during this period fell within the health laws.

Accommodation specifically provided for working women and girls represented a further development. The four decades before the first world war saw no abatement in the constant arrival into the cities of women seeking employment. By the turn of the century women had become a significant part of the wage labour force, the 1901 census finding 4,171,751 women (or 31.6 per cent of all women) in industrial and domestic employment. By the 1870s, the question of how these working girls and women were to be housed in the cities had become a matter for grave concern.

Newspapers and reports from interested associations reiterated the notion of threat to a respectable young woman's morals that this lack of accommodation was seen to present (Twining, 1876, p.76): 'I am anxious to add my testimony to the need for such "Homes for women students and ladies engaged in business as have been suggested by some of your correspondents",' wrote one early social worker to the *Woman's Gazette*. Many women put their energies into establishing homes and lodges for working women. As one argued at a Girls' Friendly Society meeting in 1878 (Girls Friendly Society, 1878):

Numbers of young women who work out-of-doors are strangers in London. Perhaps they were living as in-door apprentices or assistants in some small country town, and in an evil hour came up to London expecting to find the streets paved with gold! . . . next thing to find a home . . . . How disheartening is the almost invariable 'we don't take in no young women . . . . Our apartments are only for gentlemen'.

Homes for working girls were thus established in response to this need, and by 1882 there were 350 beds for young women in London in such accommodation, charging approximately 5s a week for a single room (2s 6d for a dormitory bed) and 4s 6d for board (Factory Inspectors Report, 1881).

However, there continued to be a massive shortage of cheap and decent accommodation. 'Respectable' lodgings could rarely be found under 12s a week (*The Times*, 1891), remaining out of reach of many working girls for whom 8s a week was a typical wage at the time. Nevertheless, by the early 1900s the numbers of residential clubs for working women, particularly in London, had increased. The accommodation ranged widely from such clubs as the Connaught Club where women paid £1 a week for board and lodging, to the Soho Club for lower paid women workers where 4s a week for a cubicle was the charge.

The most notable alternative source of housing for working women was accommodation connected with employment. Sixty-five per cent of women under twenty-five years who were employed as shop assistants were in the drapery and allied trades. The majority of these women were provided with beds in dormitories which were often locked up at night (Higgs and Hayward, 1910, p.37). The National Union of Shop Assistants advocated the abolition of this system, despite the fact that many women shop assistants supported it as a means of housing. The objections were that this system gave the employer the right to dictate how half of his employee's salary was spent (ibid., p.42). Not only that, the accommodation was frequently inadequate and over-crowded, and the lack of supervision in these large business houses was seen to encourage 'immorality'. Many reiterated the point that the low wages received by these women, inevitably made prostitution a strong temptation, particularly in the dormitories where the women were locked out for the night, if they returned even a few minutes after locking up time. How true these arguments were is open to question. Whether a working girl who had been locked out could find a bed for the night as an inexperienced prostitute, or would know where to find clients, or how much to charge, is doubtful. It is quite possible that these arguments reflect the Victorian middle classes' preoccupation with protecting sexual morality, particularly female sexual morality.

Concern was also expressed about the lack of opportunity such housing gave women to train themselves in domestic duties – a pre-requisite for their future role as wife and mother. This theme of undesirability of girls living away from 'the bosom of the family' recurs frequently in articles during this period. The only true household was held to be the nuclear family household. Thus boarding was seen by one writer as preferable to lodging since it preserved the feeling of family life which she felt should never be lost (Mason, 1888–9, p.763). Here again is the Victorian contradiction presented by girls joining the workforce and posing a threat to family life.

However, by 1910 demand for housing continued to far outstrip the available provision. As one warden in the Westminster club reported, he had been obliged to refuse 359 written applications and the same number of personal ones in one year. At a count on 15 January 1909 in London, 1,483 women were found in common lodging houses and 184 women in casual wards. In both cases the number of women was significantly smaller than the number of men in the accommodation. Higgs argued (1910) that the real proportion of homeless women was not reflected in these figures. In the case of lodging houses, women tended to make greater demands for extra comfort and better cleanliness.[3] Lodging house keepers thus responded by either raising the price for women, beyond a price they could afford, or were reluctant to take women at all. In the case of the casual ward, Higgs argued, not only did the life of a casual constantly on the move deter women, but the worse than prison treatment afforded there forced many women into prostitution. Thus her arguments represent an early recognition of the nature of provision affecting the level of demand, and the consequent hidden nature of female homelessness.

To what extent then were the radical thinkers and activists engaged in housing, homelessness and related issues during this period? Central to political struggle of course, was the suffrage movement, which encompassed a broad spectrum of belief and strategy. Before the war, the radical suffragists represented the major challenge to a limited-demand campaign for women's suffrage alone. They challenged in particular the existing property-based nature of the vote, on the basis that only the more wealthy women would have property in their own right

(Liddington and Norris, 1978, p.26). Less well-known is the earlier opposition by feminists to the law restricting married women's ownership of their own property. Although the first feminist committee was established in 1855 to promote the reform of this legislation it was not until the Married Women's Property Act of 1882, after twenty-five years of continuous agitation for reform and several failed parliamentary bills, that married women gained some measure of control over their property.

Closely related to housing and homelessness issues were the campaigns to repeal the Contagious Diseases Acts. Between 1870 and 1885 more than 900 meetings were held by the repeal campaign supporters (Sigsworth and Wyke, 1972, p.77). The Acts were fought not only from a position challenging the obvious inequity and absurdity of having laws which affected only one sex, when the diseases were clearly transmitted by both. These early feminists, particularly Josephine Butler, removed the issue from the purely moral sphere, recognizing the important links between many women's need for work and prostitution as a possible solution. Eventually the Acts were repealed, and women in lodging houses in particular, were released from at least one form of state intervention into their lives. Further, in the 1880s women began to demand better conditions at work within organizations such as the Women's Co-operative Guild and Women's Trade Union League. However, although some of these organizations, particularly the Women's Co-operative Guild, did try to improve the position of women as housewives, they did not become directly involved with housing questions.

We have seen how a radical and sympathetic current of thought existed which recognized the more structural reasons for homelessness, and thereby challenged the more blame-oriented and moralistic approach which was rife at the time. This current of opinion as it specifically relates to women's housing needs appears to have had its greatest impact in the early 1900s. In 1909, three hundred women signed a petition demanding that the London County Council should erect a hostel for women and proposing themselves as its first residents. Similar deputations took place in other cities around the country. The action culminated in the formation of the National

41

Association of Women's Lodging Houses in 1909. The objects of this Association were to link together all the individuals and organizations interested in opening and maintaining shelters and lodging houses for girls and women; to collect and disseminate information as to existing accommodation, and to campaign for further provision; and to promote legislation for the better regulation of common lodging houses and casual wards in so far as they affected women (Higgs and Hayward, 1910, p.192). Mary Higgs, one of the founder members of the Association wrote extensively and forcefully on the subject of homeless women in *Where Shall She Live?* published in 1910. The book reflects an extraordinary understanding of the problems women had to face, recognizing that women from a wide range of economic backgrounds could find themselves homeless. Her arguments range from the lack of available housing provision and the lack of well paid employment for women to the issue of domestic violence. Referring to battered women she wrote: 'Is she to continue living before the court day with the very man who ill-treated her? If not then where?' (Higgs and Hayward, 1910, p.118). She argued that women tended to make places they had to live in more homely and keep them cleaner than men, and also cared more about the lack of a proper home in their lives, since the domestic sphere received greater emphasis in their upbringing, and their fulfilment within it was considered of prime importance. This emphasis on successful homemaking was particularly important during the Victorian era. Second, Higgs stressed the importance of clean and sanitary accommodation for women since gaining employment often depended on being able to present a tidy and respectable appearance, whereas men could go for labouring jobs, for example, in dirty clothes. Higgs and Hayward (1910, p.161, 155) set her sights high:

> there shall be no town throughout the length and breadth of our land where the poor stranger woman cannot find safe shelter, a place which if her need is great, she may call 'home' . . . not until it has been effectively realised that women, have a right to settle problems arising out of industrialism, and widely affecting their own sex, will the strength of the plan for proper shelter for women at the hands of the community be realised.

The inter-war period

This long period during which homelessness was recognized as a pressing and increasing problem came to an end with the onset of the First World War. All able-bodied women were needed for war-time activities, some finding employment in the munitions factories where hostels were eventually built to accommodate them, while others were employed in the medical services. The housing of single women can hardly have seemed a priority during years fraught with wartime preoccupations. More interesting in terms of housing and women's situation within it, is the inter-war period.

First, a major consequence of the war was a vast decrease in the numbers of young men of marriageable age, leaving many young women unmarried and having to support themselves. Combined with those women left widowed by the war, the number of women on their own was greater than ever before. It was a time, therefore, when many women were looking for, and needing work, and yet, what eventuated was that women were very quickly dismissed from the labour market once war work had come to an end (Wilson, 1977, p.116); and ex-soldiers were favoured for the few jobs there were. Not only were women in the invidious position of not being able to find jobs to support themselves, the assumption was that women should return quietly to home life – even though, for many, it did not exist.

Overall the mood of the time seems to have been one of callous indifference towards women, with concern for the welfare of men – the heroes of the war – attracting greater public sympathy. This attitude was reflected, too, within homelessness provision. Chesterton (1928, p.85) wrote of the 'fear of the authorities that an ex-serviceman should be discovered bedless and starving in the streets', which she argued 'would arouse a very general indignation, and a steady fire of criticism against the powers that be'.

Second, the inter-war period represents an important stage in the changing structure of the household. During the three decades following the war, the average household size fell dramatically from 4.14 in 1921 to 3.19 in 1951 (Laslett, 1972, p.138). What this difference reflects is the consolidation of the small and privatized nuclear family unit, where cheap domestic servants for the higher income families were a luxury of the past, and where lodging gradually ceased to be such a significant practice, as young single people became able to travel more easily to work from the parental home. Of relevance to the housing of single women, was the fall in marriage age by the 1930s (Census, 1931) which meant that there were fewer women living independently and needing housing before marriage at any one time, than in the Victorian era.

This period marks the intervention of the State in the housing market to an unprecedented degree. The low level of housebuilding during the war meant an even greater housing shortage than that which existed before. Associated with this was a deterioration in house conditions and government anxiety at industrial and political unrest.

Clearly something had to be done. The private housing market could not be relied upon to solve the problem. These were the circumstances which led to a programme of state-subsidized housing on a large scale. At the end of 1918 the government gave its well-known promise of building half a million 'homes fit for heroes'. Two notions were prevalent at the time: one, that the housing crisis was temporary and merely a result of the war; the second, that the problem was more fundamental and would not be solved by private enterprise once the immediate housing crisis was over. Not surprisingly, the latter case proved true. Various forms of subsidy devised by the Housing Acts of 1919, 1923 and 1924 did not result in a sufficient increase in supply of working-class housing. For many working class people, including women with low incomes, the subsidized houses were too expensive either to rent or to buy. Building societies, as today, demanded good credit and reliable future income from prospective clients, so women whose employment was insecure and low paid, clearly would have been generally excluded. However, many working-class families of the higher income groups, and middle-class families did move into owner occupation during this period. Bowley (1945, p.83) commented that this move to new housing, 'in all senses was a logical part of the emancipation of women, an attempt to free themselves from household drudgery'. Perhaps so for the married woman, but the drudgery of single women's lives cannot have been similarly alleviated.

The major housing option for many people in the inter-war

years continued to be cheap, and hence often overcrowded, rental housing. New rent policies in the 1930s enabled local authorities to fill their vacancies with the poorer families for the first time. However, it is unlikely that many single people benefited from this shift. In Bowley's (1945, p.120) view: 'The market for local authority houses was largely confined to a limited range of income groups, that is in practice, the better-off families, the small clerks, the artisans, the better-off semi-skilled workers with small families and fairly safe jobs'.

Interestingly, however, the Housing Section of the 1931 Census discussed the need for more separate houses in terms of not only the increase in numbers of married couples and families, but it also stated that widows, widowers and divorcees under sixty-five years, and 10 per cent of the increase in single persons should be recognized. This represents an early official recognition of single peoples' housing need, which nevertheless has continued to remain entirely secondary to the housing of the nuclear family household.

How, then, did homeless women fare during the inter-war period? First, in the 1920s lodging houses remained a significant source of housing provision. For some of the reasons discussed earlier, however, this form of housing had begun to decline quite dramatically by the 1930s. A survey in 1932 found that the population of these establishments had fallen to one-sixth of the numbers in the late nineteenth century. Although social and economic conditions accounted for this decline to some extent, there is also evidence of direct discrimination against women. The London County Council, for example, ran lodging houses of reputedly decent standards for men but refused to provide similar accommodation for women, the justification being that lodging houses for women were harder to manage (Chesterton, 1928, p.162). By 1926, 9.4 per cent of the total available accommodation in public lodging houses had been licensed by the London County Council; this amounted to 1,630 beds. However, despite this licensing standards continued to be low – stained beds, dirty blankets, rudimentary washing conditions were the norm. The cost of such accommodation averaged between 1s and 1s 6d, with unlicensed doss houses providing cheaper accommodation for those who could not afford such a price.

The casual ward had become even less significant in the

post-war period. The 1930 Departmental Committee report on 'The Relief of the Casual Poor' in an investigation on one night of the casual ward population in London, and several other provincial poor law unions found 110 women as opposed to 2,472 men. Fifty-six of these women were between forty and sixty years old, and twenty-five were over sixty years, so younger women were barely using these institutions. How much these small numbers were the result of the very limited provision for women, (there was only one casual ward in London at Southwark), is impossible to ascertain. However, the report concluded that the practice of relieving women within the poor law institutions should be extended instead of special casual wards being provided.

Despite the continued existence of many of the Victorian charitable institutions and working women's clubs a shortage of decent accommodation for homeless women remained. Although homelessness appears to have diminished as a matter for public concern, some individuals still attempted to publicize the issue. Orwell (1933) is famous for his exposé of life in the casual wards and doss houses of London and Paris. Less well known is Mrs Cecil Chesterton's report. She decided to find out for herself what the life of an outcast homeless woman in London was like and in 1926 left her middle class comforts to experience life on the streets. In *In Darkest London*, where she described her experience, Chesterton expressed a similar understanding to her predecessor – Mary Higgs. Like Higgs she espouses a sympathetic attitude to prostitution and its economic base for women, and again there is a recognition of the wide range of class backgrounds from which homeless women came (Chesterton, 1928, p.29):

> Generally speaking it's poverty, and very largely, the shortage of housing, illness, bad luck, increase of rent, which drive many a decent woman out of her home and force her to become a tramp on the road, or to sell matches in the street.

Chesterton emphasized too, the severe lack of suitable housing for women that so concerned the members of the National Association of Women's Lodging Houses (ibid., 1928, p.65):

> Be they prostitute, office cleaner, or match seller – (and those from other classes) – whether they pay a few pence or a

larger sum – they all suffer from the same crying and shameful injustice; the inadequacy of accommodation, the lack of proper bathrooms, the glaring inequality which supplies the outcast male with the decencies of life and denies them to women.

Chesterton's aim, therefore, on her return to her own home after living on the streets, was to establish decent hostels for women, where they could get on their feet in an atmosphere of support and encouragement rather than shame. Thus, in 1926 the Cecil Houses (Inc.) Women's Public Lodging Houses Fund came into existence to begin to meet the need. By 1929 three houses had been established accommodating a total of 162 women and 32 babies. In these, for 1s a night, a woman could find a bed, hot bath, all facilities for washing clothes, hot tea and biscuits at night and in the morning. If a woman was in need and could not pay, the shilling was paid from a special 'Needy Fund'. The costs of these establishments were met entirely by donations and subscriptions. Other Cecil Houses were likewise established in the following decades, meeting a small part of the continuing need for housing for single women in London.

Conclusion

We saw in this chapter how the beginning of state activity in the housing market marks an overriding concern with the housing of families, with single people being left to their own devices, which has continued until the present. In the next chapter we see how many of the institutions for the homeless which still survive were established in this period, and many of the ideas which found currency in the Victorian era re-emerge at a later date. The sympathetic statements of the members of the National Association of Women's Lodging Houses are echoed in the feminist approach to the issue in the 1970s. The centrality of the Victorian family re-emerges in the post Second World War period. Women's sexuality is the focus of discussions on women's homelessness in the nineteenth century when prostitution is seen as central and in the 1970s when Brandon emphasizes women's sexual attractiveness. The notion of the deserving and undeserving poor recurs in the Housing (Homeless Persons) Act of 1977. These are but four areas of similarity.

Chapter 4

Homeless women – an historical perspective: from the Second World War until the early 1980s

It is helpful to look at the thirty-eight years since the end of the Second World War in terms of three phases. From 1945 until the early 1960s single person homelessness, and indeed homelessness in general, was not a major focus of public or radical concern. During the 1960s homelessness once again entered the public arena – its prime focus, at this time, being on families. Single homelessness during this period was perceived as essentially a male 'problem'. An analysis of attitudes, policy and practice in the 1970s reveals a shift in this respect. Despite a continuing marginalization of homelessness, an increasing recognition of the issue does emerge. This chapter is thus divided into three sections: 1945–1960s, the 1960s and the 1970s, in the recognition that those periods reflect public perceptions of, and activity around, homelessness rather than inherent differences in unmet or hidden single person housing need or homelessness at the different times.

1945 to the 1960s

The immediate post-war Labour Government faced many of the same problems of Lloyd George's government in 1919. Once again there was a severe housing shortage: hundreds of thousands of houses were destroyed or uninhabitable through bomb damage, and new housebuilding had been at a virtual standstill for six years. Thus, the first objective of the Ministry of Reconstruction was to set up a general programme for those who were seen to be in greatest housing need. From 1945 to 1948 there was an upsurge in local authority completions from 2,000 units to 190,000 (Merrett, 1979, p.239). In 1947 expenditure cuts in housing were announced, with the result that the number of municipal dwellings approved but not started fell from 101,000 to 42,000 one year later. In 1949 the Housing Act empowered local authorities to provide accommodation for any member of the community, not exclusively for 'the working classes'. Nevertheless, as in the 1920s the emphasis was on the provision of housing for the family unit.

Public housing policy continued to operate in favour of, and reinforce, nuclear family households in several ways. First, in 1946, local housing authorities under the central control of Bevan's Ministry of Health, were to decide on the number and type of dwellings to be built in their area, and to select tenants. It was stated that, 'The Government's first objective is to afford a separate dwelling for every family which desires to have one' (Ministry of Reconstruction, 1945, p.2). Authorities thus concentrated on the construction of three-bedroomed dwellings for family households, a policy which continued throughout Labour's term of office, and under the Conservatives until 1953 (MHLG, 1955). Households other than families were not mentioned in housing policy documents and reports until 1951, when 'Housing for Special Purposes' (Central Housing Advisory Committee, 1951) was published, which emphasized the 'special' housing needs of old people and single persons, rather than a more general and non-specific concept of non-family housing need. Thus, despite the fact that 11 per cent of private households in England and Wales in 1951 were one-person units, only 6.3 per cent of dwellings built by local authorities in 1953 were one-bedroomed units. In addition, more than one-third of households at this time were extended households and not 'primary family units'[1], which are likely to have included some individuals who would have chosen to live alone if housing were available, or if they had not been constrained by material or social pressures.

Second, through the combined effects of property development in the city centres pushing up land values, slum clearance and municipalization programmes, many inhabitants of the pre-war inner city were displaced to new high density, high rise blocks, or outerlying housing estates and New or Expanding Towns where land was cheaper. Traditional extended family and neighbourhood networks were broken down, leading to

49

increased isolation and a home-centred existence for many families. The ideology of these New Towns is well illustrated in advice given to the municipal tenants of a New Town developed in a later period (City of Peterborough, n.d., p.70) :

> Now that you have attained your desire of a new, soundly built modern house for yourself and family, it is perhaps an appropriate time to consider how the amenities now available to you can best be used. In the past, you may have been forced to make the best of overcrowded conditions. Do not overcrowd your family now. . . . Take advantage of all the space in your home for every aspect of daily living and family life.

The ideal was that each family home be self-contained in its own garden, common front gardens were not advocated. The effects of such policy on the provision of housing for single people are clear: there was virtually none.

The third area of housing policy where emphasis on housing for the family household is sharply revealed is the owner-occupied sector. From the early 1950s, housing policy documents of both Conservative and Labour governments reflected a notion of owner-occupation as the ideal form of tenure for the family. Of all the forms of ownership it was conceived as being 'one of the most satisfying to the individual and the most beneficial to the nation' (MHLG, 1953, p.3). Again the ideology of the family is foremost (ibid., p.17): 'Families want something better: extra room; more amenities; more pleasant surroundings. There never will be an end to the improvements which we can make in our own homes if we are prepared to work and save for them.'

Building controls had been relaxed in 1951 so there was a surge in private speculative building; a further stimulation to home ownership was the 1959 Housing Purchase and Housing Act. The overall picture from 1953–61 reveals an increase in private sector house completions from 34,000 in 1952 to 178,000 in 1961 (Housing Statistics, 1962). Moreover, state subsidy arrangements were changed so that by the end of 1956 no subsidies were available for general needs construction, except for one-bedroom dwellings for the elderly (Merrett, 1979, p.249).

It is evident from this summary of government housing policy between 1945 and the early 1960s that the housing needs of single people, with the occasional exception of the elderly, were considered marginal. This primary focus on the family in the housing arena did not, however, exist in a vacuum, it reflected the strong ideological and social pressures on women to leave the jobs they had had during the war and take up their roles as wives and mothers. As in the Victorian era, there was much discussion about family life and the important role women had to play in maintaining family unity within the home. The initial post-war period was thus one in which the numbers of women in the workforce decreased from 5,270,000 in 1945 to 4,900,000 in 1947 (Department of Employment and Productivity, 1971, Table 113). By the late 1940s women were being encouraged back into the labour market to meet the demands of post-war reconstruction, but only if 'family responsibilities' were not too time-consuming. The message was to work outside the home 'only for whatever length of time they could spare, whether full-time or part-time'; the Government was not appealing to 'women with very young children, although for those who wanted to volunteer, or who had children a little older there were many places in nurseries and creches' (Ministry of Labour, 1947). In reality, the number of nursery places was small, decreasing rapidly in the immediate post-war period, and young mothers were forced to withdraw from the labour market for at least some years, with implications for their future employment prospects. Overall, women's work remained predominantly low paid[2] and in the less unionized sectors of the labour market.

The ideology of the family, with the man as chief breadwinner and the woman as domestic labourer, thus reverted to its earlier dominance. One implication of such a climate was the concealment of women's potential homelessness. Women in unsatisfactory marriages, for example, may have chosen to remain through lack of alternatives and strong ideological pressures. This would explain the low divorce rate in comparison to earlier and later years.[3] However since concealed homelessness can only be guessed at retrospectively, the focus here is on the more visible aspects of homelessness during the late 1940s and 1950s.

Homelessness 1945 to 1950

With the exception of the immediate post-war years, this was a period when homelessness was not an issue which sparked much public concern. Government policy on homelessness was enshrined in the National Assistance Act (1948), which emphasized rehabilitation rather than institutional care. In 1948, Welfare Departments were established within local authorities as successors to the Poor Law authorities, to provide care, (including residential care in an institutional setting) of the old, infirm and handicapped. The National Assistance Act (section 21) made it 'the duty of every local authority . . . to provide . . . temporary accommodation for persons who are in urgent need thereof . . . in circumstances which could not reasonably have been foreseen . . .'

Temporary accommodation was provided for homeless families only; Welfare Departments had no statutory obligation to accept responsibility for single people who were under retirement age and not infirm.

The only statutory provision for the single homeless continued to be the casual wards which became 'reception centres' to be administered by the National Assistance Board. The new emphasis of these centres tended to be less punitive and was more one of persuading the single homeless to 'settle down' (section 17): 'It shall be the duty of the NAB to make provision whereby persons without a settled way of living may be influenced to lead a more settled way of life.'

The concept of a settled existence was based on the financial independence of single people (section 18): 'people who persistently resort to reception centres when capable of maintaining themselves must do suitable work whilst there, or otherwise be liable to imprisonment.'

This was clearly a deterrent to many women. Despite the rise in the number of female applications to the casual wards immediately after the war[4], the numbers in reception centres were low throughout this period; a report in 1952 (Ministry of National Insurance) stated that the number of women in reception centres throughout England rarely exceeded a hundred on any one night. Amongst the possible explanations are the small amount of places for women actually provided, and women's dislike of such institutions.

Other forms of housing provision for single women which had existed before the war, such as the private rented sector, common lodging houses and charitable organizations, continued to exist. The private rented sector represented approximately 50 per cent of the housing stock in 1951 (CSO, 1970, p.137) and was still at this stage a significant sector for single person housing. Common lodging houses were of decreasing importance despite being the only option for many older women. The majority of the female population in lodging houses according to one study (Laidlaw, 1956) were over sixty years old, and many were widowed. None of the charitable bodies established new hostels for homeless women during this period, although under the National Assistance Act (S20) voluntary organizations undertaking the same functions as reception centres were entitled to Board funding.

The 1950s was a period when there appears to have been comparatively little focus on the homeless. However, by the end of the decade the picture had begun to change: new legislation concerning the mentally ill (1959) and the decontrolling of rents (1957) was passed which had specific repercussions on homelessness.

1960 to 1970

In 1960 homelessness once again entered the public arena as a cause for 'moral panic'; the flurry of activity and concern which arose continued into the 1970s and resembled the concern expressed in the years before the First World War. There were several reasons for this changing climate.

The increase in the housing stock was offset by a decrease in household size, i.e. by a change in family structure, arising in part from urban renewal and housing policies which reinforced the nuclear family rather than larger households. Households were splitting into smaller units. Marital breakdown was increasing, despite the dominant ideology (reinforced by family-centred case work by social workers) that the family should stay together. The number of marital breakdowns in England and Wales, as represented by divorces granted, increased from 30,000 in 1951 to 111,000 in 1972 (CSO, 1978, p.50); the remarriage rate was also decreasing[5]. Many of these cases involved couples with no children under 16, who were likely to form two separate households ineligible for local authority housing (ibid., Table 2, p.14).

Overall the population was ageing, an increasing proportion of households being made up of single, widowed or divorced people over 60, the majority of whom were women (ibid., p.44). In the Greater London Council area single person households had almost doubled in the decade from 1961 to 1971, constituting by 1971, 24 per cent of all households (Census, 1971, GLC Small Area Statistics). It is clear, therefore, that the demand for housing by single people was increasing during the 1960s.

The situation was further exacerbated by the 1959 Mental Health Act and the later DHSS circular which advocated that mental hospital patients should be cared for in the 'community' (DHSS 37/72) which involved less immediate cost than the high cost of institutionalization. This development was facilitated by the increasing use of injectable long-lasting drugs which contained the socially unacceptable behaviour of those diagnosed as chronically mentally ill. The 'community care' facilities were, however, largely non-existent, and discharged patients found themselves homeless without any neighbourhood networks to support them. Changes in family structure, and the increase in the number of married women working outside the home, meant that ex-patients were less likely to be cared for within the family (by women in particular). As there was no concerted attempt to provide suitable permanent housing for ex-patients this homelessness proved long-term for the many who went back and forth between hospitals and the shelters for the homeless.

In addition, the private rented sector was decreasing. In 1951 there were 6,200,000 dwellings in the private rented sector (52 per cent of the housing stock); by 1961 there were 3,476,000 privately rented dwellings (31 per cent of the stock) (CSO, 1970, p.137). There were several reasons for this sharp decline: the 1957 Rent Act, which created insecurity of tenure, permitted rent rises, and opened up part of the sector to property development via conversion to owner-occupation; the expansion of finance capital into the funding of residential property which displaced the rentier petit bourgeoisie (Cowley, 1979, p.86) and massive inner city property redevelopment. This decline had serious implications for single women in need of housing, who were largely excluded, through their single status or through lack of income, from the public and owner-occupied sectors. Likewise, the decline in the numbers of lodging houses, hostels and reception centres which had started in the 1920s continued throughout the 1950s and 1960s. Between 1961 and 1971 there was a 42 per cent reduction of common lodging house beds for women (Brandon, 1973a, p.6) and nearly half the available beds for women were in London. Outside London there were no registered common lodging houses at all. A lodging house providing beds for forty-six women in Birmingham closed in 1968 when a Health Department spokesman said that 'there was no problem about homeless women' (Brandon, 1971). Again, property development in the inner cities ensured that many of the old lodging houses and hostels were demolished to make way for more profitable land use. These factors, combined with improved standards leading to less crowded dormitories in the surviving institutions, account to a large extent for the sharp decline.

The fourth notable development in the 1960s was a growing liberalization of laws affecting women (for example divorce and abortion legislation) and attitudes towards the sanctity of the family and women's position within it. The increasing number of marriages ending in divorce represents one trend. Of great importance also was the movement of married women into the labour force: in 1951 there were 7,532,000 women in paid employment and 9,045,000 by 1968 (Department of Employment and Productivity, 1971, Table 120). Clearly, this afforded married women at least some economic autonomy and threatened to a certain extent the traditional model of family life. Nevertheless, women's wages remained on average much lower than men's[6]. As the 1960s progressed the ideological climate became one of greater sexual independence which encouraged an increasing number of women to look for housing on their own away from their families. The burgeoning feminist movement of the late 1960s will be discussed later, since its impact on housing did not occur until the following decade.

The government's major concern with what was seen as an alarming rise in homelessness was the homelessness of families. Two studies were commissioned (Greve *et al.*, 1971 and Glastonbury, 1971) in which the term of reference was the analysis of the homeless in 'temporary' local authority accommodation. Single people were excluded from the studies since they were ineligible for this accommodation. The studies were thus restricted to a narrowly defined group of homeless families rather than, as their titles suggested, looking at homelessness overall. This reinforced the policy of treating single people as a special category outside the family mainstream, and indeed reinforced the invisibility of the homeless single person.

However, one government report did address itself to the single homeless, ('Homeless Single Persons', NAB, 1966), although again the definition of homeless was restricted to those sleeping rough, including those who used lodging houses, hostels and reception centres. Men outnumbered women overwhelmingly in the survey; of the total population using such accommodation (28,789) it was estimated that only 6.6 per cent (1,905) were women. The apparent unequal sex ratio was not analysed as an interesting or illuminating factor in itself, instead, women disappeared from any analysis of the results or were briefly mentioned at the end. The emphasis was on the deviant characteristics of the homeless, rather than on issues such as housing shortage. No one questioned the validity of the low estimation of women's homelessness, nor recognized the importance of strong social and economic pressures keeping women in the home, or their increasing reliance on tranquillizing drugs. Neither was there any recognition of specific reasons, such as fear of violence or the stigma attached, as to why women would be less likely to sleep rough than men, or why existing hostel provision was inadequate to suit their needs. By concentrating on the single homeless as a special group, their homelessness was defined as a welfare problem – divorced from any economic analysis involving income levels or housing shortage. By concentrating on those sleeping rough, the numerous concealed homeless – often women, were ignored and homelessness appeared as a smaller problem than it actually must have been. Government housing policy continued to be based on the notion of the family household with state housing for those households, predominantly families, who could not afford home ownership, the 'ideal' form of tenure.

In the voluntary sector, the early 1960s marked a revival of interest in homelessness which led to the initiation of many new projects. The Simon Community was one of the first and was fairly typical. The idea behind it was to bring 'Community social work and psychiatric principles to the meths drinker and the homeless isolate' (Brandon, 1973a, p.7). The 'problem' was perceived as homelessness amongst the young in Central London. The Simon Community aimed to 'reach out' to these people rather than wait for them to approach institutions, by which time they would be long-term vagrants. Initial contact was made through soup runs, supported by day centres and hostel provision. The workers were non-professionals committed to the breakdown of the worker/resident barrier.

The majority of the new provision was mixed, reflecting the liberalization of moral/sexual attitudes. In the event, the small mixed hostels often did not accept women, as staff were reluctant to admit one woman alone, and two or more were rarely referred simultaneously. It was not until some years after the emergence of the new wave of concern about single homelessness that the housing needs of homeless women began to be recognized by some organizations. Christian Action – a radical Christian organization – became aware of women's homelessness when it found that approximately one third of the people sleeping rough in Waterloo Station in 1965–6 were female (Brandon, 1971, p.5). Having perceived a need for an open-door hostel for the care and rehabilitation of the most destitute and disturbed women who were rejected by organizations like the Church and Salvation Army, Christian Action opened a shelter in Lambeth in 1967. The demand for beds in the small terraced house was constant and the need to expand became quickly apparent (Brandon 1969, p.7):

> Even though the house was stuffed full of homeless women, there was incessant knocking at the door and the police, probation service or local authority social workers telephoned trying to find beds for people. We turned away more and more women each month.

The emphasis was on creating a short-term refuge run on community psychiatric principles with social work support for any woman who had nowhere to go. Autonomy, self-reliance and independence were encouraged. Later the emphasis changed to one of greater social diagnosis and individual treatment, recognizing the need for the treatment of serious psychological difficulties and providing more than 'just a roof'. Other voluntary projects took similar action and established small, open-door refuges for women acknowledging that many homeless women did not come into contact with the male-oriented hostels, day-centres and soup runs. Younger women, often homeless through family upheaval and 'emotional instability', were seen to have urgent needs, and were considered easier to encourage to settle down. Long-term homeless women who had been drifting for years were thought to need substantial help and care before they could re-establish a more settled way of living. Consequently, the different organizations tried to adapt their hostels to accommodate specific needs.

The central government response was to fund agencies according to the categories of homeless people that had been identified. For example, the DHSS funded projects for alcoholics and drug-addicts,[7] and (with local social service departments) for ex-psychiatric patients. The DHSS also acted as a source of indirect funding by paying the rents of the residents on state benefits. Due to the large numbers of unemployed residents, the payment of benefits to cover their rents represented substantial financial support to the projects.

Government departments argued about who was responsible for funding which category of homeless people, thereby diverting discussions from challenging more fundamental issues of housing shortage. The long-term homeless, who were seen as 'sick beyond treatment', were regarded by central government as the responsibility of local authority social service departments, who were supposed to care for the old and chronically mentally ill. By the late 1960s the Supplementary Benefits Commission was becoming concerned that its own Reception Centres and the voluntary residential projects it funded were becoming dumping grounds for the long-term homeless, the chronically ill and the handicapped, for which the centres were not intended and were not suitable. This left the workers unable to perform their designated task of 'resettling' the homeless residents. The SBC therefore wanted other welfare services to take on the 'unsettleable', but statutory local authority 'homes' tended to be restricted to those needing very specialized care. Likewise, local authority funding to voluntary organizations tended to be available only to projects providing sheltered housing for similar groups.

The dominant ideology of the new homelessness projects was akin to that of Christian Action. Staff stressed the need for more than shelter, and aimed to recognize the basic unsatisfied human needs amongst their homeless clients, and to provide short-term 'treatment' programmes within a sheltered residential setting with a high staff/resident ratio. Since many of the residents were ex-mental hospital patients, who were being discharged in line with government policy, the approach was clearly useful. Likewise the emphasis on self-determination and independence was important for many of the ex-patients who were often unable to live autonomously after long periods of enforced passivity and institutionalization.

Increased interest in homeless women at this time was due not only to the increase in the amount of visible female homelessness[8], but also because their behaviour was less tolerated. Although they were a numerically smaller group they were seen to be more likely to be seriously disturbed than their male counterparts. Women alcoholics were seen as more dangerous, uncontrollable and unpredictable than male alcoholics, whose drunkenness or violence appeared more normal and thus acceptable (Otto, 1980). Personal factors were seen as being of overriding importance in women's homelessness, to the extent that a specific female homelessness 'model' was constructed[9]. According to Brandon (1971) homeless women between the ages of sixteen and thirty were sexual deviants, mainly lesbians and frequently addicted to drugs! Women were described as more emotional than men with strong needs for love, protection and dependency. In leaving these needs unfulfilled, independence in women was seen as leading to delinquency in the young and madness in older women! Sexuality, ignored in relation to men's homelessness, was once again considered central to definitions of homeless women, although the focus had changed from 'moral concern' to one where women's need to prove sexual attractiveness was considered paramount (Brandon, 1971).

In conclusion, the emphasis of the 1960s was on the deviance of the homeless – a pathology model. This distracted attention from structural changes such as the increase in single person household formation and the decrease in the private rented sector and in relation to women specifically, from the significance of their position within the family, the labour market and the housing market. It was not until the 1970s that feminists began to challenge this perspective.

59

The 1970s

Early in the 1970s the Government acknowledged homelessness as a growing problem. According to the Parliamentary Undersecretary of State for the Environment: 'it was not possible even for the government' to estimate homelessness figures, but that numbers were increasing (Hansard, 1971, p.169). More people were thought to be sleeping rough; in Inner London estimates were as many as 11,000 people (ibid). How much this reflects merely a shift from hidden to publicly visible homelessness, and to what extent this represents a real increase in homelessness, is difficult to ascertain. The indications are, however, that single homelessness was growing.

Housing developments and demographic and social changes

There was a sharp rise in housing land and construction costs in the early 1970s (Merrett, 1979, p.263). By 1970 public house-building had been cut back by local authorities as a response to the constant pressure from central government to decrease public expenditure: public housing starts were at a lower level in 1970 than at any time since 1962. This decline continued unevenly throughout the 1970s as the economic crisis brought further cuts in state expenditure on housing, which from 1977 onwards were particularly acute. The general trend was towards rehabilitation and municipalization away from redevelopment, but the costs involved often meant that houses stood empty for many years. Increasingly the public sector was becoming a residual sector for low-income family households who could not afford home ownership.

Council house sales to private individuals were promoted by the Conservative administration which came into power in 1970. In addition the Housing Finance Act of 1972 changed the system of council rent subsidies to place more emphasis on rent rebates for low income tenants and less on blanket subsidies; this made home-ownership, subsidized through tax relief, a more attractive proposition to better-off tenants. In the early part of the 1970s demand for owner-occupied housing grew, matched by an expansion of private sector construction. Owner-occupation continued to be promoted by the two major political parties; however, it was still not a feasible option for many low income households, including single women. By 1980 an average house or flat cost £23,000 (£29,000 in London) whereas the average male wage was only £6,000 a year, and for women, £4,000 (New Earnings Survey, 1980). Finally, the private rented sector continued to decline at a critical rate, falling from 19 per cent of the housing stock in England and Wales in 1971 to 13 per cent of the stock in 1980 (CSO, 1981(a), p.74).

Household formation was still increasing due to the ageing of the population and other social changes affecting family life. People were marrying at an older age. The divorce rate continued to rise, with a greater number of divorces being petitioned by women. The implication of these factors was that more women on their own were in housing need. Yet women's inferior economic position meant that they tended to be at a greater disadvantage than men in the private housing market. Despite the Equal Pay Act 1975 women's wages were only 58 per cent of men's wages in 1976. The number of women registered[10] as unemployed soared from 106,000 in 1971 to 414,000 in 1979. In contrast the number of men registered as unemployed rose from 618,000 to 930,000 in the same period (DE, 1980).

A further significant development was the growth of the women's liberation movement. The expansion of higher education amongst women as well as men, economic prosperity and the changing social and sexual mores of the 1960s had led to a notion that equality had been achieved in society. This was in fact illusory, the reality for women who were in the labour market, often in low-status, low paid work, and carrying out most of the domestic work within the home, led to feelings of oppression. Women began to voice these in the early 1970s. Through the feminist movement women encouraged and supported each other in their demands for autonomy and independence. Practical help was given to women living in intolerable domestic situations, who wanted to leave – particularly women suffering domestic violence. This changing climate affected the nature of the voluntary provision for the homeless which developed in the 1970s.

The response from the non-statutory agencies

The impact of non-statutory organizations and groups on government policy in the 1970s was substantial. The large emergency hostels in London and common lodging houses continued to decline throughout the decade[11]. Fewer than a dozen of the remaining hostels were for women, most of these housing between thirty and sixty women, as compared with the men's hostels which often housed from 200 to over 1,000. Voluntary projects for women tended to favour the provision of housing in smaller hostels, with separate rooms and communal facilities for women who wanted some degree of companionship and support. Some organizations were influenced by a growing feminist perspective (Homeless Action, 1977–8, p.5): 'There has been a tendency to regard homelessness among single people as a consequence of individual failure, rather than a failure of successive government legislation to provide accommodation for anybody except those in nuclear families.'

Often in the past voluntary projects had focused primarily on providing emotional care and support, and had been prepared to accept grossly inadequate and overcrowded premises. Now, material conditions were increasingly seen as important to the well-being and 'rehabilitation' of the single homeless. Some hostels were non-specialist, simply housing people in need and stressing the autonomy and independence of residents; others were specialist, providing support and care for particular homeless groups (alcoholics or the mentally ill).

The growing current of radical opinion was that the focus should be on the physical lack of suitable housing for single people rather than on the characteristics of homeless individuals. It was recognized that this housing shortage affected the most vulnerable groups first, but that the single homeless were not simply those with 'problems' other than housing problems. As one agency wrote, single people were 'no more or less likely [than families] to have additional social problems, beyond their lack of a place where they (had) a right to sleep' (After Six, 1974, p.4). There was a questioning of the use of 'single' as a special category, aside from the family mainstream, in light of the growing proportion of single person households especially in Inner London (DHSS 1975, p.22). The distinction between single homeless and homeless families was recognized as a false one, arising from previous policy rather than from recognizable differences between the two groups (After Six, 1974, p.4):

> The distinction . . . is a purely bureaucratic one. Central and local government have decided, for reasons of scarce resources and priorities, that only the very young, families where there are dependent children, and the very old, the sick and the lame, can be 'statutorily homeless' and eligible for direct local authority help. For anyone [else] the prospects are very different, though their situation may appear exactly the same.

The women's aid movement challenged the sanctity of the family providing refuge and housing for women who were fleeing from violent boyfriends or husbands. The possibility of housing for women and their children became a real one, although single battered women often had greater difficulty obtaining accommodation. Likewise standard definitions of single homelessness were expanded by some voluntary organizations to include the concealed homeless. It was recognized that there were immense difficulties in estimating the numbers of these hidden homeless single people since they had little incentive to sign on council waiting lists, and were often deliberately discouraged from doing so by housing officials. It was not until 1980 that Shelter estimated the number of concealed single person households as 1.3 million using figures from the 1977 National Dwelling and Housing Survey (Shelter, 1980, p.6).

Finally, the squatting movement which encompassed many thousands of single women and men represented a significant political resistance by homeless people to the situation they faced. Squatting in empty premises (usually owned by the local authority) throughout the major cities in England was made possible by the extensive municipalization programmes of the early and mid-1970s. Local authorities bought houses and flats which, due to financial and bureaucratic constraints, they often failed to rehabilitate for many months or years. Single people objecting to the lack of affordable rented housing and their exclusion from access to local authority housing squatted these houses. Local and national squatting associations were formed, conferences held, campaigns launched, and mass resistances were organized against evictions. For the first half of the decade, many single women and men found housing in this way. Central and local government were forced to respond.

The picture then bears similarities with the period before the First World War; many of the radical and feminist attitudes of the earlier period are echoed in the 1970s. The effect of these groups on government policy was, however, very different, reflecting the different role of the central government in the housing market which had developed throughout the century.

Central Government policy

In 1972 a survey of the situation in lodging houses and hostels was commissioned by the Department of Health and Social Security. Although this survey (OPCS, 1976) extended the definition of single homelessness to include the institutionalized homeless it did not fundamentally alter the restricted nature of the definition. The 1972 survey illuminates the implications of such definitions for women's homelessness and its concealed nature. Headcounts of hostel residents were taken as indices of housing need, and since women represented only 8 per cent of the hostel population, the conclusion was that this percentage accurately reflected the numbers of women who were homeless, and that women's homelessness was therefore not very significant.

This opinion was modified as the 1970s progressed. Government working parties were established to examine what was seen as the wider problem of single people's housing needs. These included authorities with responsibilities for housing such as the DOE, the GLC and the LBA as well as the DHSS. Attitudes expressed in these reports reflect a notable change in perspective (GLC and LBA, 1975, p.30):

> The single homeless are not simply those with 'problems' of one kind or another other than housing problems . . . the evidence is overwhelmingly that the major cause of homelessness among single people. . . is a shortage of accommodation at prices they can afford.

The recommendations centred on the notion that greater responsibility should be taken by statutory housing departments in the form of grant aid, subsidies and a range of hostel and housing provision. Administration should be rationalized, and where additional care and support was necessary there was to be closer collaboration between housing and social services agencies. It was recognized that hostels should not be seen as the major provision and were generally only suitable as temporary accommodation. It was recommended that permanent accommodation should be provided which included self-contained flats as well as group housing with more, or less communal versus individual space according to residents' preferences (GLC and LBA 1977). The influence of the voluntary sector on these reports is clear.

Central and local government response to most of these proposals was to ignore them. Overall the housing needs of the single homeless continued to be neglected. The 1974 Housing (Finance) Act, the Housing (Homeless Persons) Act 1977 and 'special' local authority schemes for the single homeless are the notable exceptions.

Under the Housing (Finance) Act 1974 housing associations[12] that registered with the Housing Corporation (an arm of the DOE) were eligible for Housing Association Grants, state loan funding was available from the Housing Corporation or local authority housing departments for buying, converting and maintaining properties, to be paid back through the 'fair' rents (set by a rent officer) paid by the tenants. Between 1974 and 1980 housing association stock doubled to approximately 2 per cent of the total housing stock in England and Wales, and 3.7 per cent of the stock in Greater London (GLC, 1981, Table 1).

Housing associations were heralded by the Government as the major future provision for the single homeless. The Housing Association Grant was to be the main channel for state funding for provision where the primary need was for housing as opposed to care. It was intended to take the place of the myriad of central government welfare provisions; in cases where care was the major element, resources were to be provided by local authority social services departments. Housing associations were more amenable to housing single people than local authorities because they were not bound by duties under the housing acts in the same way. Many voluntary agencies, therefore, took advantage of this new development to expand their provision for the homeless. Through a combination of hostels, group homes, and self-contained units, a range of provision deemed to suit the 'special needs' of the single homeless was established. A central concept of this provision was to establish stages of housing along a continuum, with increasing self-containment as the 'special needs' of the residents subsided. Thus the institutionalized were given the opportunity of becoming gradually more autonomous in small, shared houses usually of a high physical standard.

Housing associations did not, however, provide housing for the majority of single people. Resources tended to be channelled towards families and 'special needs' groups. At least 50 per cent of lettings (rising to 100 per cent in certain areas depending on local authority policy) were used by the local authority to house people from the council waiting list, using the points system which virtually excluded single people under the age of sixty. The only exceptions to this local authority nomination system were specialist housing associations, the majority of which housed groups defined as vulnerable under the Housing (Homeless Persons) Act. The allocation policy for the remaining lets, in line with government guidelines, tended to concentrate on the 'priority groups' defined by government legislation; these were old people and specific need groups like the disabled. Thus the National Dwelling and Housing Survey (DOE, 1978) revealed that approximately 50 per cent of all households in housing associations consisted of persons aged over sixty, and only 16 per cent of people under sixty without children; 'special needs' groups accounted for a further 7 per cent.

The Housing (Homeless Persons) Act represented the major statutory response to the growing concern with the homelessness problem.[13] The Act imposed a duty on local authorities to provide housing for people who could prove that they were 'unintentionally homeless' if they were in 'priority need' of accommodation and had a 'local connection'. As indicated earlier, the Act was primarily intended for those with dependent children, the notion of vulnerability – the criterion for the rehousing of homeless single people – clearly serving to marginalize single peoples' homelessness. The Act also emphasized the role of the voluntary organizations, as opposed to statutory ones, in providing accommodation for the single. Local authorities were empowered to give financial and other assistance to such bodies.

Rather than dealing directly with single homeless individuals as part of the standard allocation procedure, many local authority housing departments favoured the setting aside of small fixed quotas of lettings on an annual basis to their own social services departments, or to local voluntary organizations working with the homeless. These bodies then allocated individual units within their quota of lettings as they saw fit. This system reinforced the notion of agencies having to provide care and support to the single homeless and to act as mediators between housing departments and their 'clients'. Moreover, such a policy provides a special avenue for the institutionalized homeless and those in touch with social work agencies, which is denied to the concealed homeless – many of whom are women. Nevertheless, a significant aspect of the Act was the shifting of the responsibility for housing the homeless from the social services departments to housing departments,[14] which represented a recognition that homelessness was primarily a housing and not a social problem.

The most important point about the Act was the economic context in which it was passed. The Act was brought into force at a time when Britain was suffering severe effects of economic recession. By 1977 in Britain the gross domestic product was below the 1973–4 level in real terms; there had been successive cutbacks, in current spending on public housing since 1976, and capital expenditure (on new and renovated housing) in the public sector (including housing associations) had fallen in real terms every year since 1975. The crucial point, therefore, was that there was a wide gap between the intentions of the Act and the resources provided to meet its requirements. Inevitably the result of the situation was an increased hostility towards the homeless. They were seen to be 'jumping the queue' of those people in 'real housing need' on the waiting list, they were the new scroungers and rent evaders. The right wing elements of the media had a hey-day.

'Special' DOE and local authority schemes

Although the DOE and local authorities intervened in the 1970s to house single people, single person housing continued to be regarded as 'special'. Moreover, this intervention was seen as advantageous to the needs of families, whose housing needs remained the primary concern (DOE, 1976):

> ignoring the needs of the single has repercussions on other groups. Many single people are living alone in homes which were once their parents' and are now too large for them to cope with and better suited to family use. Other single people live in groups in rented houses where they outprice family breadwinners . . . so the provision of accommodation for single people has advantages for the community as a whole.

The Leicester scheme was set up by the DOE as an experiment in producing dwellings for single working people. There were three sorts of shared furnished flats for the young and mobile, and two-roomed unfurnished flats built to Parker Morris standards for the middle-aged more permanent tenants. Similar 'special' schemes were built in Hillingdon and Norwich but these provided rare examples of a short-lived optimism. As expenditure on public housing was cut back, innovative plans for single person housing were the first to go.

The local authorities who responded to the massive increase[15] in single person applications to their waiting lists and to the growing number of squatters in their areas, did so in a variety of ways. Some councils offered licences to squatters who were living in empty property which they were unable to convert quickly. This became known as the short-life housing movement and was an important source of housing (frequently of poor quality) for many single people. Towards the latter half of the 1970s in order to gain access to permanent housing many of these groups formed themselves into co-ops – a specific form of self-managed housing association which is eligible for public funding from the Housing Corporation. The second major intervention by local authorities was the establishment of 'hard-to-let' schemes, which enabled single people to gain access to flats, often in tower blocks or unmodernized estates, which families were unwilling to accept. Inherent in the scheme was the notion that single people could, and should be prepared to accept any housing they were offered, and that their need for decent housing was entirely secondary to the housing need for families. For the local authorities it provided a way of filling flats which were often only acceptable to people who were in desperate housing need.

The current situation

Despite the inadequacy of the housing options available to single women, and single people generally in the 1970s, there was a certain degree of flexibility within the housing system which had decreased dramatically by the end of the decade. The election of the Conservative Government in 1979 hastened a process which was already underway – the amount of public expenditure in housing declined at an even greater rate. In material terms this meant that 106,019 local authority dwellings were completed in the first nine months of 1977 as opposed to 70,420 in 1980 (DOE, 1978, p.1 and 1981a, p.1). New house and flat construction underway in this same period reflects an even more dramatic decline, with approximately one third of the number of new dwellings begun in 1980 compared to 1977 (ibid.) Council house sales virtually quadrupled in the same period as a result of the incentive to buy with a massive discount (a policy enshrined in the 1980 Housing Act) (DOE, 1981a, p.46–51; 1979, p.47–52), and the numbers of households registered on the housing waiting lists have continued to rise. Inevitably, such a high demand for a limited stock has meant that only those households considered to be in greatest housing need have been allocated housing. Not surprisingly, single person households rarely fall into this category, indeed such dramatic cuts have only served to further increase the marginalization of single people in the public housing sector. Such schemes as did exist for single people have come to a halt, and in some cases have been completely dismantled. Neither have housing associations been in a position to intervene to remedy the situation, since cuts have likewise been administered to housing association finance.

Within this gloomy scenario voluntary groups have continued to criticize government housing policy towards single people, to campaign for a greater range of housing and to demand that single people be guaranteed equal priority with other households for the allocation of public housing. Similarly groups have campaigned to amend the Housing (Homeless Persons) Act to include all homeless people, demanding that restrictions relating to priority groups, 'unintentionally homeless' and local connections be removed. Monitoring of the Act by the Joint Charities Group indicated that restricted as its terms were, even these were not being put into practice. Vulnerable groups with the exception of the elderly, were frequently being refused acceptance as priority need groups. In 1980 only 14 per cent of homeless households who were given accommodation by local authorities were accepted because of vulnerability while the overwhelming majority (81 per cent) accepted were families (DOE, 1982a). However, the DOE (1982b) review of the Act recommended against amending the primary legislation, neither removing the concept 'of priority housing need' nor widening its definition of 'priority need' to include any other groups of homeless people without dependent children. Instead, the DOE has maintained that other recent government measures benefit single homeless people, for example, low cost home ownership and schemes to increase availability of short-term rented accommodation. There is no available evidence to substantiate these claims. This, therefore, was the situation in the early 1980s when the interviews with 160 homeless single women in London took place.

Conclusion

There are several interesting conclusions to be drawn from this historical analysis. First, ideologies and definitions of homelessness have changed over time -- in one period the emphasis was on the homeless individual as blameworthy, at another homelessness was perceived as deriving from wider economic and social structures. In line with these different ideologies, actions taken to remedy the situation have also changed. Second, despite the changing nature of homelessness, consistent themes emerge; for example, the notion of the 'undeserving' and 'deserving' homeless, the perceived relation between homelessness, women and sexuality, and the intervention by voluntary and religious bodies to provide accommodation for the homeless. Third, the historical analysis makes clear that women's homelessness can be more fully understood in the context of sexual division of labour and ideological pressures on women to conform to their role as housewife and mother. Finally, housing policy and provision, with the exception of non-statutory intervention, has always been focused primarily on the nuclear family with the consequent marginalization of single people. This theme is the subject of the next chapter.

CHAPTER 5

The family and housing: the marginalization of single households

The marginalization of single person households and single homelessness needs to be understood in the context of the dominance of the nuclear family unit. We have hitherto traced the development of this process historically and the way in which women's homelessness has been compounded by their role within the family, their lower economic status, and the scarcity of accommodation for single women. Here we further explore the themes discussed in the previous two chapters. We examine perceptions of family households and how these differ from those of single headed households, how a particular form of the family household dominates housing production and allocation and the implications of this dominance for other forms of households and the nature of specific ideologies about single people which explain the marginal nature of single-person housing provision. We focus on hostel provision since this form of accommodation has traditionally been deemed suitable for single people and thus illustrates traditional conceptions of single peoples' housing needs. The second section explores the concept of the centrality of the family to housing policy and provision at a more theoretical level.

The historical picture of women's homelessness revealed the social and moral concern about single women's lack of housing on the one hand, and, on the other, the notion, particularly in the public sector, that the housing need of the family household should be the focus of attention and policy. The predominant emphasis on the family has resulted in single person and family households being judged and evaluated according to quite different criteria. Thus, for example the Parker Morris report (MHLG, 1961, p.8) stated:

71

> Family homes have to cater for a way of life that is much
> more complex than in smaller households. . . . The design
> must be such as to provide reasonable individual and group
> privacy as well as facilities for family life as part of a
> community of friends and relations.

The implicit assumption here is that smaller households, or
people living alone, do not exist in a social world which should
affect the design of their accommodation. Instead, for many
single persons 'the self-contained bed-sitting room dwelling is
likely to continue to be acceptable' (ibid., p.13). Overall, no
consideration of flexibility and changing needs through the
life-cycle is incorporated in housing policy.

Moreover, non-family households are frequently overlooked
in the literature, or at best subsumed in the data on families in
research. This approach predominates despite the divergence
between demographic data and the normative concept of the
household. The fact that 70 per cent of households are not
composed of traditional two-parent headed family composition
with dependent children (CSO, 1983, p.24) is consistently overlooked. Even in research which focuses on allocation and access
to council housing, terms such as 'people', 'families', etc. are used
with little clear differentiation between household types. The
result is that not only is the dominant family ideology reinforced
but that an interesting dimension is ignored – the recognition of
which would often inform both the argument and the results.
The assumption of male household head or rather male consumer of housing is also prevalent.

Rex and Moore's (1967, p.273) critique of the social distribution of housing opportunities, for example, while emphasizing
the class struggle inherent in housing allocation, assumes a
male head of household also:

> there is a class struggle over the use of houses and this class
> struggle is the central process of the city as a social unit . . .
> men in the same labour market may come to have
> differential degrees of access to housing.

A specific notion of the family is contained within the system
of housing production and allocation. Kitchens are designed
with only enough space for one person to work comfortably on

the assumption that this work need not be shared. Department of the Environment design manuals and bulletins tend to portray a female figure, the housewife, in this domestic role. The workshop, garage or study, i.e. the extra leisure space associated with the dwelling, is conceived as being the man's territory (Francis, 1980). Likewise communal or more collective arrangements are noticeably absent or rare. Thus certain relations of reproduction of labour power, and a particular form of the nuclear family and the sexual division of labour are embodied within these reports. Further, the assumption that a man should support his family, and women's financial dependence on men, has meant that until recently it has been customary for tenancies in the public and private sectors to be granted to the adult male member of the household (DHSS, 1974, p.375)[1].

It is not only single households who are affected by the orientation of the public sector to nuclear families. Families who do not conform to the stereotype suffer in the housing market. The Finer Report (DHSS, 1974, p. 381) found that single-parent families were discriminated against in local authority housing. It was shown that points systems were disadvantageous to these families; in particular, schemes which gave points for overcrowding and bedroom deficiency. It is common for single parents to be expected to share a bedroom with a child whereas two parents are not. Similarly, single parent families lose out on residential qualifications, since they move house more frequently than other families, and go to stay temporarily with friends or relatives in other areas while looking for accommodation, thereby losing their place on the housing list. Other evidence revealed discrimination towards single parent families on 'moralistic' grounds (ibid., p.382):

> the underlying philosophy seemed to be that council tenancies were to be given only to those who 'deserved' them and that the 'most deserving' should get the best houses. Thus unmarried mothers, cohabitees, 'dirty' families and transients tended to be grouped together as 'undesirable'. Moral rectitude, social conformity, clean living and a 'clean' rent book on occasion seemed to be essential qualifications for eligibility – at least for new houses.

Instead, single parents tend to be allocated housing on the worst

73

estates with little chance of a transfer (Gray, 1979, ch.8).

Owner-occupation

Single-headed households – particularly female-headed house-holds – have difficulty entering the owner-occupied sector on several counts. First, the high cost of housing relative to average income means two incomes are frequently necessary to sustain the costs of a mortgage, particularly in the early years. Second, although this practice is now changing, building-societies have traditionally been reluctant to lend to groups of single people on the assumption that such a household formation is not a stable one. Third, women's lower economic status both in terms of income (women's average full-time weekly earnings are approximately 63 per cent of men's (*New Earnings Survey*, 1983)), and employment prospects, mean female-headed households, particularly those where the woman is in her forties or fifties have difficulty in obtaining mortgages. Further, there is some evidence to suggest that building-societies have tended to discriminate against women who are 'career-oriented' or who are divorced or separated (Duncan, 1976, p.6). Thus, it is no surprise to find that in 1981 DOE figures on mortgage completions show that the sex of the sole or first named applicants for mortgages is female in only 10 per cent of cases (see Table 5.1).

Even where married women are earning more than their husbands the evidence suggests that a high proportion of building societies discriminate against married applicants for joint mortgages where there is a higher earning wife (Equal Opportunities Commission, 1978). Thus, for the majority of women the route to secure housing in this sector is through dependence on a male partner, further reinforcing women's financial and material dependence on men. Since mortgage tax relief accrues to the mortgagor, where the man is the sole mortgagor, as is the case in the majority of sole mortgages, the female partner in the household is dependent on the male to redistribute this hidden income subsidy to the rest of the household. Yet the potential structural inequality and lack of redistribution of resources within households, can mean that such a subsidy only benefits the wage-earner of the household.

Second, the high cost of owner-occupation can give rise to the

Table 5.1 Summary of Mortgage Completions

Average income and sex of sole or first named applicant

		Average Income (£)	Male No.	Female No.
1969	GLC	2156	1664	72
	United Kingdom	1760	19752	611
1975	GLC	4831	1903	167
	United Kingdom	4036	26661	1182
1981	GLC	10502	2419	451
	United Kingdom	8637	27078	2691

Source: DOE, Survey of Building Society Mortgages Annual Table 1969, 1975, 1981.

necessity for women to enter employment to 'help' pay the mortgage, this has specific implications (Berry, 1981, p.9):

> the promise of owner-occupation has encouraged the growth of two-income families and the willingness of women, in particular, to accept the very worst jobs . . . this has not led to a corresponding redefinition of domestic economic roles. The symmetrical family has not arrived. Instead wage-earning women are forced to bear the main burden of domestic labour in addition to their paid jobs, the housing situation has intensified the exploitation of women, helping to add a proletarian status in the capitalist labour market to their continuing proletarian status in the home.

There is also a close ideological association between owner-occupation, or rather 'owning your own home', and an implied domestic role for women. The ideal home with the ideal house-wife choosing the furniture and fittings, and providing a warm and comfortable environment for her family is an all-pervasive scenario reflected in the popular media and literature (Rose, 1980). This ideology is central to the male worker too, as well as to his wife. Cockburn (1983) in her study of the male craft workers in the print unions found the notion of a man supporting his wife in the home, and the threat to this that unemployment posed, to be an important one. Yet the same kinds of images do not pertain to an equivalent extent to public sector housing. Likewise, increased suburbanization which goes hand in hand with the rise in owner-occupation has particular implications for women, often meaning, for example, increased isolation and a separation from the centres of employment and services (McDowell, 1983).

Single person housing

Single person housing is treated in two ways. First, it is seen and discussed in relation to families, who are defined as the priority. As mentioned earlier, it is not unusual for government policy in relation to single people to be articulated in terms of the benefits it implies for the family (DOE, 1976, p.2):

> New public sector building for these people [the young mobile] as indeed for older single people living on in large family houses will often release accommodation, either in the private or the public sector for family use so that, while being directly beneficial for single people . . . this activity can result in benefits for families also.

In contrast, housing policy directed towards alleviating the housing need of families is never expressed in terms of the benefits which may accrue to single people. Housing for single people is only provided in periods when the housing needs of families are seen to be met, or when there is a surplus in some section of the housing stock which cannot be used for households whose needs are considered of greater priority. Thus we saw how the enthusiasm in the 1970s for innovative schemes for providing accommodation for single people, such as the Leicester, Hillingdon and Norwich experiments, evaporated as the cuts in housing expenditure in the latter part of the decade served to exclude these households once again.

Not only is housing for single people not a priority; there is also a notion that single-person housing is provided for a distinct category of people who have definable, specific, and to an extent, peculiar needs. Despite demographic trends indicating that older people constitute an increasing proportion of the single population, 'single' is widely associated with the young and mobile – those who have not 'yet' formed family units for

76

themselves. Thus, the range of accommodation provided is commonly referred to as 'special needs' housing, and value-laden statements abound (Funnell, 1973, p.103): 'Single people don't need gardens – they are quite happy in flats. They don't even need balconies ... [they] go out most evenings, and go away many weekends. Their friends are rarely the neighbours.' In the local authority sector the fact that flats which are hard to let to families are let to single people with often no attempt to improve the quality of the accommodation beforehand has specific implications. It derives from the view that single people do not deserve decent public housing, and should therefore be content with whatever they are offered. Likewise, single people are expected to fend for themselves, for they are transitory, mobile and young. If the property is in a bad state of repair the assumption is that the tenant will be capable, willing and sufficiently wealthy, with enough time, to repair and maintain it themselves. Clearly there is a limited number of single people for whom hard-to-lets offer a viable housing option. If the issues of lack of supply, safety and adequate transport associated with hard-to-lets are also addressed, the number of women, in particular, for whom hard-to-lets are a possibility is further restricted.

The allocation of short-life housing to single people embodies similar notions. Housing that awaits rehabilitation or repair is, by definition, of very poor standard and often lacks even the most basic of amenities such as electricity or a fully operating plumbing system. Yet this housing is often deemed suitable for single people. Again, the assumption is that single people have the resources, financial, physical and material, as well as the skills necessary to put the accommodation into a habitable state.[2] Because single people's needs for security and stability are not recognized, they are expected to move on when the rehabilitation gets under way, for the house or flat to be eventually allocated to a household considered to be in greater housing need, most commonly the family. The single person has little choice but to accept these conditions, not because they are acceptable, but because there are few alternatives.

Private rented sector, housing associations, co-operatives and hostels

Until recently many single people could find accommodation in the private rented sector, even though the accommodation might be poorly maintained, lacking amenities, insecure, over-crowded or expensive. However, with the sharp decrease in the private rented stock this sector has become less and less of a viable housing option. Since rents tend to be high, and deposits are usually required, those on low incomes or supplementary benefits are likely to be excluded.

Nevertheless the private rented sector is still the major source of housing for the non-nuclear family household. Housing in this sector, however, was rarely produced or designed for specific households, since almost all households (90 per cent) rented their accommodation at the turn of the century. The consumption of private rented housing obviously has shifted over time, but this has related as much to changing tenure structure overall, as to changes internal to the sector such as rent levels, standards and specific pieces of legislation. Thus, it would be difficult to argue that the private rented sector embodies specific ideologies relating to household structure. Some landlords prefer one kind of tenant, some another, although the major criterion in all cases is the ability to pay.

In contrast, housing associations and co-operatives were seen by central government in the 1970s as the major provision for homeless single person households. Although housing associations mainly house similar types of households to local authorities, they do house a higher proportion of single or two person households as loan funding arrangements have encouraged the production of small dwelling units. The formation of housing co-operatives also provided an avenue to secure and permanent housing for single people, particularly many of those who were involved in the squatting movements of the early 1970s. Because tenants in co-operatives collectively manage their own property, co-operatives even more than housing associations represent the notion of self-help which is promoted whenever single person housing is discussed.

One end of the continuum of housing provision for single people is hostels. These hostels embody more than any other form of provision for this group, particular social relations and specific notions about single person housing needs. There are three categories of non-specialist hostels for single people, each of which operate according to different rules and assumptions. The first category consists of large direct-access hostels which accept homeless people who arrive at the door without having contacted the hostel beforehand, without references and (sometimes) without money. In London there are approximately 760 beds for women (Austerberry and Watson, 1983, p.16) and over 6,000 beds for men (GLC and LBA, 1981, p.16) in such hostels. The majority are run by voluntary charitable or religious organizations. Some receive statutory funding through the DHSS, the DOE, the Home Office or the local authority. Others are run entirely by charities or religious bodies and reception centres[3] (of which there is only one for women) which are run statutorily by the SBC.

Three specific aspects of these hostels interested us. The first is the rent. Contrary to a common-sense mythology, that a minimal level of accommodation would be associated with a low rent, rents in these hostels are high, at an average of £27 per week for a bed with no meals or simply breakfast, and from £25–£40 for full or half board in 1981. The implications of these high housing costs, is that homeless people are liable to be paying a greater proportion of their income, if employed, than the average expenditure (£20) of households nationally (Family Expenditure Survey, 1981, p.10).[4] Thus, at an end of the housing tenure continuum – outright owner-occupation, weekly housing costs (excluding the repair and maintenance element) are low and at the other – hostels, they tend to be high. Because hostels negotiate with the DHSS, the rents of those on supplementary benefit are paid at a higher ceiling than the standard level for rent allowances in other rented housing. For hostel women particularly, whose employment prospects are in the low paid sector, to have their rent paid by supplementary benefit and to remain unemployed, represents the only feasible option.

Second, the implications of direct access or open-door hostel accommodation for the lives of the residents are important. Because many hostels, notably the better quality hostels, restrict access on the basis of age and employment, people who are simply unemployed and older may have no choice but to live in

79

this accommodation. However, due to lack of alternative provision, these hostels also provide a roof for other people who have no adequate alternatives: those who have been discharged (sometimes prematurely) from mental hospital, alcoholics, or drug addicts. In contrast to the former group, these individuals frequently need support, and can be disruptive to the rest of the community. This range of disparate needs on the part of the residents, legitimates the tendency for hostel life to be bound by rules and regulations, designed to restrict the behaviour of a minority of residents; for example, alcohol is usually banned from the premises, and bathroom doors cannot be locked to prevent residents drowning themselves. Thus, everyone is compelled to live at the lowest common denominator of the most disruptive or disturbed, when a drink might mellow the harsh reality of hostel life, or a locked door can allow a degree of solitude and privacy where these are at a premium.

Third, the conditions of these hostels derive from material as well as ideological considerations. Due to lack of adequate funding voluntary hostels tend to be in a poor physical state of repair and overcrowded. In the majority communual sitting-rooms are large and bare with lino covered floors and furniture only found in institutions – plastic covered upright armchairs lining the walls. Privacy in sleeping arrangements is rare and dormitory accommodation, occasionally curtained off into cubicles, is the norm. Similarly, self-catering is seldom allowed and canteen meals are provided. The minority of hostels permit visitors, and there is never any space conducive to entertaining a relative, friend or lover. The expression of human needs for privacy, self-expression, personal tastes and sexual relations is entirely excluded; the constraints militating against these are too great. The lack of policy at a statutory or individual hostel level to remedy this baseline level of existence implies an assumption that homeless people do not have these needs, or that these needs do not have to be taken seriously.

The second category of hostels providing accommodation for single people can be defined by their small size. These are refuges, group homes and open-access hostels. The majority of these are for women, having been established by feminists in the 1970s who were influenced by the ideology of self-help developed in the women's liberation movement. The first are predominantly for battered women and their children, and women without children in refuges tend to be in the minority. Most refuges in England are members of the Women's Aid Federation England, and are run according to feminist principles. Women are encouraged to determine their own lives, and make their own decisions with the support of each other and the refuge workers, who are usually non-resident. Group homes are run on similar principles by voluntary organizations who obtain good standard converted accommodation from housing associations to manage themselves. The women in this form of accommodation usually have security of tenure and their own rooms, and self-catering facilities are provided. The residents are encouraged to participate in creating a group atmosphere within the house, and prospective residents are interviewed and only accepted if it is thought that they will 'fit in' with the rest of the household. Finally a small number of hostels with only five to twenty beds accept many of the same homeless people who go to direct-access hostels. In London there are five 'women only' and thirty-four mixed small open-access hostels providing fifty-five beds for young women and 114 beds with no age restriction (Austerberry and Watson, 1983, p.20). There are no published figures on the number of beds for men in these hostels. There are no residential staff in this form of accommodation and again residents are encouraged to live autonomously as much as possible.

The third category of provision can be identified as the 'up-market' hostels. These hostels have their origins in the Victorian period and represent a significant source of accommodation for women on their own, particularly in London where there are approximately 8,000 beds for women in sixty women-only and ninety-five mixed hostels (ibid.). There are no available figures on the number of up-market hostels for men but inspection of the files of a housing advice agency for single people revealed that there were very few. Acceptance is restricted to students, low-paid workers and travellers, and frequently to people under thirty. Only one-quarter of the beds in the 'up-market' hostels for women in London do not restrict admission on the basis of age, but even many of these are orientated towards younger women. Rents are frequently high (ranging from £20–£70 per week for a single room), which clearly excludes very low-paid workers or people who are employed

81

intermittently. Although hostel residents are eligible for means tested rent allowances the initial claiming procedure takes several weeks and allowances do not cover staff and service costs but the rent element alone. Underlying the criteria for admission into the accommodation for women only is the notion that these hostels are for the 'respectable working woman', which derives from their original conception in the early 1900s. With rising female unemployment, some hostels have begun to accept unemployed women who appear 'respectable', 'educated' or 'middle-class' as long as they exhibit no signs of 'having problems'.

The physical standard of accommodation in the up-market hostels tends to be good. Residents in the long-stay hostels are frequently provided with their own bed-sitting rooms, and self-catering facilities. Nevertheless, the lack of space in the rooms militates against residents having their own furniture or bulky possessions. Usually there is one single bed, a bedside chair, a built-in wardrobe, desk or dressing-table and a sink – rooms for solitary use and not for entertaining in. Communal areas are arranged formally, with rows of chairs directed towards a wall-mounted television and floors polished to an impersonal shine. The physical form of the provision reflects two notions. One is that single people's need for social relationships, particularly sexual relationships, barely exist, and in so far as they do exist, an institutionalized communal space can meet these needs. Thus, although the single rooms with their locked doors do permit some form of privacy, the restricted space and institutional regulations make a viable social life impossible. Second, most of the hostel wardens interviewed in the 'women-only' hostels were frightened that the lack of rules and regulations would necessarily imply chaos and anarchy. Closely tied in with this fear is an emphasis on the question of sexual morality and the need to contain and delimit female sexuality which again relates to their conception in the Victorian era. The result is that a boarding-school atmosphere pervades many of these institutions.

It is clear then that the hostel accommodation which is provided reflects assumptions about how single people and women particularly, ought to live be it autonomously, co-operatively, celibately, or institutionally. It would appear that by its very nature hostel provision is inevitably founded on certain principles or assumptions. On a pragmatic basis alone, the size of the household or population accommodated, makes the simple provision of housing within a hostel, with no definition of lifestyle attached, an unusual phenomenon.

Why this centrality of the family to housing?

So far the discussion of the marginalization of single person households and the centrality of the nuclear family has focused on allocation, access and existing provision. Given the apparent centrality of the nuclear family in housing and the implications of this for women, it is interesting to examine what theorists have made of the centrality of this structure. Perhaps the most remarkable feature to note is that many writers actually reinforce this dominant family model in their own work. With the exception of some recent feminist work (see for example, McDowell, 1983; Rose, 1980) the literature notably lacks an analysis of how patriarchal and capitalist social relations are articulated in housing.

The centrality of the family can conceptually be theorized at different levels. According to an institutional analysis, management needs – the desire to minimize rent arrears and disruptive social behaviour – the beliefs, assumptions and prejudices of managers are important in determining which households are accommodated and the quality of tenancy offered. Another fairly common explanation for the exclusion of single people is that there is an absence of a large stock of small dwellings considered suitable for single households (Gray, 1979, p.216). On a similarly 'pragmatic' note local and central government representatives justify the virtual exclusion of single people from council housing in terms of the limited stock available, and the necessity, first and foremost, of providing accommodation for children – and of course, for those responsible for them.

Although such an approach raises some relevant issues, it does not go far enough. Why is the ideology that non-traditional households tend to be disruptive a pervasive one, and why is there less housing for single people? An analysis of the dominance of the family model to housing might be better understood in the context of capitalist and patriarchal relations. Several writers have adopted a broadly Marxist framework in their analysis of state intervention in the housing sphere, but these writers have not incorporated a feminist analysis into their framework. Magri (1972) for example, has argued that the housing crisis of the late nineteenth century, characterized by high rent levels, overcrowding and little new house construction, presented problems for the reproduction of a large section of the labour force. The State intervened, according to Magri, to encourage the building of cheap single family units through local authority housing agencies, to set space standards suitable for single family households and to keep rents low. Moreover, she stressed the significance of housing provision in establishing stable family units which she argued were a necessary requirement for the reproduction of labour power at this time. Also in the context of France, Pincon (1976, p.178) argued that state housing specifically 'benefits as a priority the labour power which is most precious for capital' and for the 'functioning . . . of the state apparatus'. Those workers whose incomes are too low to enable them to reproduce themselves adequately in the private housing market are thus provided with housing as a social or indirect wage.

Although these writers begin to raise some important questions, there are clearly problems with such an analysis as it stands. As Pickvance (1980, p.42) has noted, there is no evidence to substantiate Pincon's explanation that the State intervenes to provide housing for particular categories of labour. What is needed is an analysis of which sections of labour are most useful to capital and evidence that these groups cannot gain access on their own behalf to housing, and that social housing reduces housing costs and improves the quality of housing for the workers in question. Likewise, Magri's argument that labour power was not being adequately reproduced because of the housing crisis needs proper investigation. One approach might be to examine sickness amongst workers at the time, the level of productivity of workers, the rate of turnover of workers etc. (Pickvance, 1976, p.74) which would give some indication of the extent to which labour was being adequately reproduced or not.

Several British writers (Ginsburg, 1979; Merrett, 1979) have also attempted to locate state intervention in housing within an analysis of capital and the balance of class forces. Merrett (1979, p.61) argues that state housing after the First World War was seen by capitalists and the Conservative Party as a means not only of reproducing the capacity to labour, but also of 'securing the perceived legitmacy of the social order'. For the working class on the other hand, public housing provided a means for advancing their material interests. These kinds of analyses are useful and clearly to fully understand the role of state intervention in facilitating the reproduction of labour power, would require detailed analysis of the social, economic and class forces at the relevant time. The problem however with such Marxist analysis is that although it posits some relation between the need to reproduce labour power and to maintain social order, it cannot explain why housing for the family household specifically is the predominant form of provision. At the very least Marxists need to examine the family and familial ideology. This may force Marxists to consider the strength of feminist writings on gender relations.

Barrett (1980) and Barrett and McIntosh (1982) have usefully explored sociological Marxist and feminist explanations of the primacy of the nuclear family form. We do not intend to intervene here in the debate on the family but simply to point to some developments in Marxist, feminist and Marxist feminist theory which might help us understand the dominant ideology of familialism in housing. To date little attention has been paid in this debate to the role of housing. Marxists have argued that the traditional family is useful to capitalism in that it represents a mechanism for the inheritance of private property and a system for the 'cheap' reproduction of labour power where women do unpaid domestic labour as well as existing as an industrial reserve army of labour to be exploited in waged labour when necessary. Further, it is argued that the traditional privatized family form creates the illusion that there is a sphere of individual emotions and interaction which is not penetrated by market relations and that this facilitates the political acquiescence of the working class (Bruegel, 1978). The family can also be theorized as a significant consumption outlet where goods that could be shared are bought individually. If we relate these arguments to housing provision, the contention that the family (and hence in this context, family housing) benefits capital as a cheap and effective method of reproducing labour power does not hold. If workers are housed in barracks, rather than in an individual family home, with their costs of reproduction borne elsewhere as in the South African apartheid system, the total costs in reproducing the working class would clearly be lower (Barrett, 1980, p.221). Arguments concerning the privatized nature of the family might, however, be useful in explaining the predominant individualized form of housing produced for the family household – a form which is in such direct contrast to the impersonal and 'collective' housing provided for more marginalized groups as we saw earlier. As for arguments relating to consumption, individual housing units clearly do act as an outlet for capital to first build and then to penetrate. Row upon row of family houses and flats are duplicated each with their own washing machines, dishwashers, vacuum cleaners, ovens and freezers. If a form of housing was produced which enabled a more rational and collective use of resources, fewer commodities would be demanded in individual consumption units and hence fewer could be produced.

Feminists have raised further important questions, of which we shall note two here. First, it is argued that the family is a significant site in the construction of gender identity – from which all men can benefit in societies where masculinity is associated with certain sorts of advantages. Second, men are seen to benefit from the patriarchal nature of the family since it represents the site of male control and a place where men can enjoy the domestic service and comfort provided by a largely dependent wife. The importance of family housing to the first argument is questionable. Gender identity can be learned in a variety of contexts and it is not clear that housing plays a significant role. However, it is clear that the privatized nature of the family home, under the man's control, fits in with this kind of analysis. Such an explanation would also be endorsed by the lack of challenge by the trade unions, representing the more powerful sections of the male working class, to the traditional form of housing produced, and by the absence of trade union demands for more housing for non-family households. The role of the State is also important since, as has been explored in the context of welfare provision (Wilson, 1977), the State has played a significant part in actively supporting and constructing the family unit and the dominant family ideology.

Through analyses which recognize the importance of looking

86

at housing in the context of the specific class and social forces of the time we can begin to explain how the traditional family has come to be so central to housing in Britain. Of importance also is the fact that the marginalization of single-headed households derives from their lack of political strength and coherence as a group which militates against the possibility of any substantial gains being made. Individuals often move in and out of the 'single' person status throughout their life-cycle, and it is this particularly which contributes to their lack of visibility and coherence as a social group. Although the housing needs of single old people may differ from those of students or the divorced woman in her fifties, the fact that these different forms of housing need are marginalized derives from the same source, that is, the centrality of the nuclear family to housing. Further, the fact that these housing needs are experienced individually with no defined material base for shared collective action across groups, further reinforces the powerlessness of single households. Workers who face redundancy can collectively struggle at the point of production against employment. Single individuals and non-traditional households who are about to become homeless rarely have an equivalent base, except in cases such as the mass evictions of squatters or the closure of an institutional form of provision, around which they can organize. The historical analysis showed how there has been no strong pressure, except at brief historical moments, for single people's housing needs to be taken seriously. The consensus has been to let the single fend for themselves. For those who have the income needed to house themselves in the private sector or the fortune to be housed in the public or voluntary sectors, there is no problem. For the single who lack income, or who occupy a weak position in the labour market, it is a different question. Through lack of alternatives these single people take jobs with accommodation provided or stay in domestic situations or intolerable housing circumstances against their choice. We argue that women constitute a significant (although unquantifiable) proportion of this group. It is to the experience of single homeless women to which we now turn.

Part II

CHAPTER 6

Experiences and definitions of homelessness – the women's viewpoint

This chapter returns to one of the first questions raised in the book – how to define homelessness – with a focus here on the meaning of homelessness from the homeless women's viewpoint. Through the women's definitions we can explore further two themes developed earlier: first the notion of the home-to-homelessness continuum and the relativity of any definition of homelessness; and second the significance of the sexual division of labour in understanding the meanings attributed by the women to the concepts of the 'home' and 'homelessness'. Of the four questions designed to investigate the women's definitions of the 'home' and 'homelessness', two were open-ended. The first two came in the housing section in the early part of the interview. These were: 'Do you consider your present accommodation to be your home?' and 'If so, what is it about it which makes you describe it as a home?' 'If not, how would you describe a home?' The second set of questions came in the section on the women's social situation towards the end of the interview, These were: 'Do you think of yourself as being homeless?' and 'What does the word homeless mean to you?' We hoped that the time lapse between the two questions would mean that the women's response to the questions on the home would no longer be in the forefront of her mind and would thus not strongly influence her response to the homelessness questions.

The home to homelessness continuum

The complexity of the home-to-homelessness continuum is clearly illustrated by an interesting contradiction revealed in the responses given to the first part of the two pairs of questions. If a

91

straightforward definition of 'being homeless' as being equivalent to 'being without a home' is assumed, a consistent relation between the answers to the two questions would logically follow. Thus, if a woman said that she did not consider her present accommodation to be her home, it would follow that she would consider herself to be homeless. Likewise, if a woman did consider her present accommodation to be her home, we would not expect her to say that she thought of herself as homeless. However, we have argued that no such straightforward definitions of the 'home' and 'homelessness' are possible, and thus such a consistency should not be assumed.

The women's responses support this contention. We found that 30 per cent of the women who did not consider their present accommodation to be their home did not define themselves as being homeless. Similarly, 32 per cent of the women who considered their present accommodation to be their home thought of themselves as homeless. It is apparent, therefore, that many of the women did not equate the notion of homelessness with being without accommodation that they defined as 'home'.

We can gain a greater understanding of this contradiction by analysing the women's responses to the two open-ended questions, that is, to the meanings that they attributed to the concept of the home and homelessness. Since homelessness is a relative concept and has to be defined in terms of such factors as the conditions and standard of the physical structure, and the nature of actual and possible social relations within the physical structure, we examine the different meanings attributed to the home under five categories: material conditions and standards, emotional and physical well-being, social relations, control and privacy, the 'here and now'.

The home

Smart and Smart (1978, p.6) wrote:

> The ideology of women's place being in the home has served to perpetuate the existing sexual division of labour and to effectively limit the forms of women's participation in the public domain . . . making a withdrawal into, and a predominant pre-occupation with, or concern for, the home and family seem natural for woman.

This is an important context for understanding the definitions of the 'home' which follow.

Material conditions and standards

The majority of the women interviewed emphasized the significance of decent material conditions and standards in their definitions. Many women specifically mentioned the furniture and interior fixtures of the house:

'A home is a nice fireplace and grate, nice radio playing, a fitted carpet, and a three piece suite and a table in the corner for your dinner, and that's it.'

'A home is where it is kept clean. I like nice wallpaper. I like the sitting room done every two years, the bedroom every three years. I like a cosy place.'

'It's got to have some identity of yours, where you can put your furniture, and hang your belongings, and where you had some permanence – give it some of your own imprint, paint it and so on. I'm paying off for something I'll never have.'

A woman living in a bedsit said:

'I call this a cage. I think I've lowered my demands – I grew up in a four bedroomed house – but I still want a self-contained flat with my own kitchen and bathroom.'

'A furnished place isn't a home. I'd like an unfurnished flat, then I could buy little pieces from the shops and make it into a home.'

'A nice sitting-room. A clean carpet. Walls clean, toilet very clean, carpets and kitchen floors polished, linen washed every week, and cooking a routine job every day. A real home would have a garden too.'

This emphasis on the interior of the dwelling is interesting since it reflects the fact that women traditionally are more actively involved in defining the internal domestic sphere, and have greater control over this aspect of housing than over any other sphere.

93

Emotional and physical well-being

For many women the concept of a home was strongly associated with a sense of emotional well-being. A sense of comfort, warmth and security was felt to be of prime importance. Safety was frequently mentioned, particularly by the women in women's aid centres who had fled for refuge from domestic violence. Home is:

'Somewhere you feel happy, contented and safe. Somewhere that is nice to go home to. My place is not a home. I feel frightened – it's where my husband died. My house[1] feels eerie. It has been broken into three times. I can't bear to be there.'

'A base, somewhere you feel at ease. Where you can be your own person. A home is peace of mind.'

'Somewhere I felt comfortable and happy to go back to after work. Happy to be alone. Here I just feel that I have to be out all the time. I really hate it.'

Social relations

For other women the nature of social relations that existed within the home was of greater importance. Not surprisingly, the dominant ideology of the 'happy housewife' shone through in some of the responses. Home is:

'A family.'

'A home is happiness with your husband going out to work, and you're at home doing the shopping and cooking, and you can come home, sit down, watch telly and have a cup of tea.'

'I associate my parents with home.'

'A proper home is with your own relations.'

'Someone to care for, and someone to care for me. Somewhere you're loved. Warmth.'

There is an interesting similarity here between these definitions of the 'home', and Brandon's (1973a) emphasis on the family as central to the concept of the home discussed earlier.

The second important aspect of social relations within the home expressed by the women was the possibility of entertaining friends at home. Since women traditionally socialize at home rather than in public spaces many considered this to be a central part of their lives:

> 'A home would be my own little place where I could buy things and make it nice, where I could invite my friends back for a cup of tea.'

Another woman living in nurses' accommodation said:

> 'All I want is a one-bedroomed flat where I can ask friends around. You can't have friends come and sit in your bedroom here – it's no life.'

Control and privacy

A strong element in the majority of homeless women's conceptions of home is the notion of controlling one's own life within it, not subject to other peoples' whims or, in the case of hostels, the institutional rules and regulations. Closely linked to this is the concept of privacy, the option to act as you choose within the confines of your own four walls. This theme has been prevalent in the notion of the home, since the Victorian era, as the historical analysis showed. Many women focused on these issues. Home is:

> 'Somewhere that I have my own keys to and I can be private in – have my own things so I don't always have to share with someone.'

> 'Somewhere I know I've got my front door key to come and go as I please. I'll consider it home when I have my own toilet and bathroom and don't share it with 30 other people.'

> 'Where you can eat what and when you want, not at set mealtimes, come and go as you like, and watch any programmes you choose to on T.V. and not have to go to bed at 10.30 when all the good programmes come on.'

> 'Somewhere I can do my own thing without harassment and interference.'

'A place where I can choose the decor, and where who comes and goes is my choice only. Somewhere I can control the environment. Home is one's own place, it allows one's own tastes to flow out and then come back to you – to enjoy. It's very essential to women. You don't really feel a woman, without a nest. It's the expansion of your personality. It's such a joy to arrange things, the colours and the textures.'

'Here and now'

We have grouped together the last set of statements under this heading to denote the attitude of a minority of women who were so accustomed to their homelessness that they considered anywhere they currently lived or slept as home. Most of the women who expressed this tenuous notion of home were women who had been homeless or who had not lived in secure accommodation for a very long time. For them home was:

'my little plastic bag'

'anywhere I hang my hat at this stage'

'I've got to the stage in my life, where home is just wherever I am.'

Two points need to be made in conclusion. First, there is clearly an ideological content as well as a material base to many women's conception of home. For all the reasons which we have already discussed, this is not surprising. For many women, control over the domestic and privatized sphere may constitute the only area of control and influence in their lives. Many constraints on women prevent their active participation in the public sphere, and in the labour market particularly. The lack of a home in this sense thus has a particular meaning for women. If a woman does not live in accommodation which she considers to be home, it may well mean that she feels that she has lost the one area of control women traditionally can have.

Second, the facilities, conditions and standards that the women desired were not extraordinary. Wanting one's own room, privacy, autonomy, reasonable cooking and washing facilities is not 'unreasonable'. Indeed, in the case of the nuclear family household such standards are not only generally accepted as desirable they are recognized in government surveys and circulars. An extract from the Parker Morris Committee's report (MHLG, 1961, p.8) illustrates the way that perceptions as to the 'necessary' characteristics of the home internally, vary according to whom the dwelling is to be for:

> Family homes have to cater for a way of life that is much more complex than in smaller households. . . . At every stage in life of the family the home has to provide for an extremely wide range of activities; and even when the bedrooms come to be put to wider daytime and evening use, living areas in the family home will still be in use for children's play, homework, watching television, sewing and mending, hobbies, entertaining friends.

Furthermore:

> many married couples will require larger accommodation because they wish to have a spare room so that friends, or children who have left home, will be able to visit them.

For single households, on the other hand, there are no such possibilities: 'We believe that the self-contained bed-sitting room dwelling is likely to continue to be acceptable' (ibid., p.13).

Homelessness

The definitions the women gave of homelessness counterpose the definitions given for the home. They could be categorized as: poor material conditions, lack of emotional and physical well-being, lack of social relations, lack of control and privacy, and finally, at the extreme end of the home-homelessness continuum – no roof.

Poor material conditions

Poor material conditions were an important focus of many of the women's definitions of homelessness:

> 'Homelessness is living in a dilapidated, damp and run-down building with broken windows.'

> 'Homelessness is not having a permanent base. I still have

my belongings scattered everywhere. I have no control over the decoration and the furniture. My identity isn't printed on the place, the space is very restricted – it curtails my activities, I can't have friends to stay.'

'Homelessness is always wandering, always moving and never buying things you want because moving is such a hassle. Always changing your address and having to let people know.'

'No locks on the bedroom doors or bathroom even.'

'Homelessness is when everything is dirty. Nothing is clean anywhere.'

'Homelessness is nowhere to put your personal belongings – things that mean a lot to a single person. You can't express yourself in your furnishings as an individual. It's an affluent age and you feel like you're on the outside looking in. I look at people shopping for groceries and I envy them being able to plan for meals and cook for themselves and for their friends. When people at work talk about buying stuff and making their homes nice I never say anything any more. It would be different in India or somewhere, but here you're brought up to expect to have a place of your own.'

The last woman's comment expresses the social and cultural determination of the concept of homelessness: she would have felt differently had she been living in India, her country of birth.

Lack of emotional and physical well-being

The lack of emotional well-being that homelessness and insecurity of housing tenure imply was a constant theme:

'Destitute. Despair. Finished. If you're feeling those things you really feel your life's not worth living and you may as well be dead.'

'I feel nameless. I feel I don't exist. I'm just a thing. That's what I feel like living here.'

'You lose interest in things – you feel powerless and victimised.'

'It makes me feel very insecure. A base is very important. I don't like moving around a lot. It's difficult to extend yourself outwards with no secure base socially and at work.'

'Homelessness is desperation. You've got nowhere at all. The thought of it frightens me.'

Mental illness is relevant in this context. Many studies of the homeless (see DHSS, 1976; Drake *et al.*, 1981) have found a high incidence of mental illness history. In the DHSS survey, for example, 30 per cent of the women mentioned mental, physical or social problems. We also addressed the issue. Our view is that the results do not represent an entirely accurate picture of the mental illness/homelessness relationship, or of the rate of incidence of mental problems. This is partly because some of the women were reluctant to answer these questions because they experienced them as intrusive, and partly because this kind of information is notoriously difficult to obtain and unreliable (Drake, *et al.*, 1981, p.36). Nevertheless, the information collected gives some indication of the connection between homelessness and mental illness. To fully establish the extent to which homelessness was a cause or effect of mental problems would require more extensive research methods (for example the use of psychiatric reports) than the ones used. However, mental illness, anxiety and depression appear to be a result of homelessness in as many instances as they are a cause. Since there are considerable social pressures on women to be successful wives and mothers in the home, the lack of a home is liable to become a source of great anxiety and depression.

While recognizing that the data collected is not perfect, it supported this hypothesis. Approximately one-third of women had been treated for mental problems,[2] the majority of whom were living in the direct-access hostels.

Housing and domestic problems were seen by the women as the main 'triggers' of mental problems, with housing problems being given as the central reason by 64 per cent of the concealed homeless group who had been treated. Many of those for whom marital and family problems were the trigger for mental problems (85 per cent and 70 per cent respectively) had also lost secure housing due to marital or family disputes. Second, the loss of housing or homelessness was reported by thirty-two women as an important factor in exacerbating or causing many of the problems.

'I'm certain I'm as ill as I am because I have nowhere to go. It's progressively worse since I've had nowhere to live.'

'When you're homeless and jobless you feel psychologically insecure, you begin to develop a nervous tension. I think it's harder for a woman than for a man. Women are more emotional.'

'I get very depressed. I expect people to do things for me. I get uptight, I take it out on my friends.'

'I used to get so depressed in my bedsit. So lonely. All on my own in an area I didn't know. I'm sure it was living there that ended me up in hospital.'

Age

A significant component in the lack of emotional well-being is associated with age. For men in this society, particularly men of the middle and upper classes, maturity and age often means a good job and a position of stability. Women likewise have expectations of a secure home and stability as they get older; they often do not expect or want to be on the move at this stage. Yet for many women the reality does not fulfil their expectations. As Simone de Beauvoir (1949, p.595–6) so aptly expressed it:

Towards 50 she is in full possession of her powers; she feels she is rich in experience; that is the age at which men attain their highest positions, their most important posts; as for her, she is put into retirement. She has been taught only to devote herself to someone and nobody wants her devotion anymore. Useless, unjustified, she mutters: 'no one needs me'.

Age was an important issue for some of the older women.

'Homelessness makes me feel very bad, especially at my age [57] when most people are married and have their own home. I have nobody, no brothers or sisters you see.'

100

'Being homeless makes people feel bad. I used to get terribly depressed. I used to hide in corners and cry. It's not very easy to start all over again at my age [61]; that's why I'd prefer a bedsit. You'd have everything you wanted there. I couldn't set up my own place again.'

'I feel I'm at an age [58] when I ought to do something. It's difficult to move from the hostel after being here so long.'

'When I'm feeling sorry for myself I feel homeless, because it's connected with my expectations. I'd imagined I'd be settled and have a home when I was 50. But I feel homeless with reservations – because I'm here – it's more connected with the divorce – the idea of homelessness.'

'I worry about where I'll be when I'm 70. Still living in hostels I suppose.'

Lack of social relations, control and privacy

Several of the preceding remarks illustrate the connection between homelessness and notions of family and marriage. This is an interesting connection which we explored by comparing the homelessness definitions of the ever-married and never-married women. A much higher proportion of the women in the former group (53 per cent) saw themselves as homeless than in the latter group (37 per cent). This suggests that women who had been married, having once shared accommodation with their husbands, had higher expectations of a home and gave more emphasis to the significance of social relations within it, than the other women. Since these aspects were lacking in their lives they were more likely to experience themselves as homeless. The other important 'social' side of homelessness mentioned was the inability to conduct social or sexual relationships in private and invite friends home. These aspects were similarly articulated in the women's concept of home.

In the same way as control and privacy are relevant elements in the definition of home, so their absence is a significant part of definitions of homelessness for women. The hostel residents in particular mentioned this aspect of homelessness frequently:

'Homelessness is being in a hostel or flatshare. Somewhere not your own. Somewhere you don't want to be, where you have no security of tenure, where you have to live by other peoples' rules and can't do what you want.'

'Homelessness is when you have nowhere to live and somebody puts you up for a few weeks. Nowhere to rest yourself privately. It affects people, not seeing your friends, not being able to do your own thing and cook your own food.'

'To be homeless is to be unable to switch off the light when you want. Cough when you want. Get up when you want. It makes you feel terribly degraded. You couldn't get lower than that.'

No roof

The notion of homelessness as being without a roof with literally nowhere to go, was the most commonly held definition – 38 per cent of the women expressed this concept of homelessness in various ways. This is not surprising. Sleeping rough with nowhere to go is at the extreme end of the homelessness-home continuum and is what literal homelessness is generally assumed to imply. The media and literary[3] image of the homeless person consistently focuses on such an image. The concept was articulated as follows:

'No roof. A seat bench.'

'Streets and floorboards. Panic and upset. It horrifies me.'

'Walking the streets. People who've got nowhere to go and don't know where the next penny is coming from.'

'When you're sleeping under wood or sleeping underground – or wherever you can sleep.'

'Homelessness means you're pushed from one place to the other, and you can't sleep out in the streets because it's too cold.'

'Nowhere to put my head down. Under the stars.'

The contradictory response

The paradoxical nature of the womens' responses raised earlier can be understood in the context of the range of definitions given. The two final categories of definition of home and homelessness – which we called the 'here and now' and 'no roof' categories respectively – clearly represent the most extreme minimalist definitions of the words that could be given. The two contradictory sets of responses – 'No, I do not consider this accommodation to be home and I do not think of myself as homeless' and 'Yes, I do consider this accommodation to be home, and yes I do think of myself as homeless' – hinge on these minimalist definitions. The women who did not consider their present accommodation to be their home were making this judgment on the basis of some subset of criteria discussed above – emotional and physical well-being, social relations, material conditions, and control and privacy. The lack of one or more of these meant that they did not consider their accommodation to be home. In contrast, they also held the minimal notion of homelessness – the no roof definition – and because they were not literally on the streets, they did not consider themselves homeless. The reverse goes for the second set of contradictory responses. The women who considered their present accom-modation to be home did so because they considered anywhere they currently slept, as home. On the other hand, they also thought of themselves as homeless because their concept of the word was broader than simply having no roof over their heads or nowhere to go.

An analysis of the quantitative data supports this hypothesis, showing that 80 per cent of the women who did not think of themselves as homeless associated homelessness with having no roof over one's head. In contrast only 9 per cent of the women who described themselves as homeless used this definition, these women predominantly defined homelessness in terms of notions of 'privacy', a 'home of your own', a 'place where you could do as you wanted' and so on.

Some ambivalent responses to these questions illuminate the picture further:

'I really have to confront the whole thing. I look over at the

Sally Army hostel and think, I'll move in there. What is the difference between me and someone there? It's only an attitude of mind that makes me different from a wino. It doesn't do to dwell on it.'

'Homelessness is little old men going around with bags over their shoes. So to that extent I don't think of myself as homeless. Shelter bills – the stereotype. But the only reason I'm not *actually* homeless is because the people I'm living with are too middle-class to fling me on the street.'

'I'm not homeless in terms of people who have real need, but I feel that I am in a way. I feel very disoriented.'

'Homeless? I am in a way. I mean I'm in a hostel – not having a place I could call home. You have to leave this place when you're 60 – so I'm homeless in the sense that it's not for my retirement.'

In conclusion, this analysis has clearly illustrated the difficulty of drawing a line between having a home and being homeless. This difficulty is further compounded when discussing women's homelessness, because the sexual division of labour in this society implies a specific domestic role for women, and thus a specific meaning of the home, as the women's definition showed. We argued earlier that definitions of homelessness and the way homelessness is perceived have implications for policy and provision. Definitions of homelessness also have implications for the homeless individual herself in terms of what actions she will take to alleviate, remedy or fight against her situation.

We explored this further by asking the women how they perceived other peoples' attitudes towards homelessness generally and their own homelessness specifically. In response, some women emphasized negative and unsympathetic attitudes, reflecting the Victorian notion of the undeserving poor, who have only themselves to blame, the notion that homelessness can be intentional as enshrined in the Housing (Homeless Persons) Act 1977, and so on. Others considered people to be broadly sympathetic and understanding, echoing the early social reformers' concern with the lack of decent affordable housing and the notion in the 1970s that homelessness derives from inequalities in the housing system, rather than from the psychology of the individual. Yet, others thought that both negative and positive attitudes were prevalent. Homeless women's families and friends also viewed the situation in a variety of ways, some blaming the individual woman for her lack of decent housing, others giving sympathy and support. The following comments reflect the range of responses given:

> 'I think the homeless are regarded as industrial waste, you have the strong and the weak, and in a society like ours, some just don't make it.'

> 'They're depicted as squatters or shown up as spongers almost. Rubbish, just poor souls. Monsters.'

> 'They look on them as losers, people who don't try and haven't tried. To be compassionate you have to have experienced the situation. They think homeless people can't have come from a good background.'

> 'The authorities don't care, or do anything about it. The press don't report it enough, or show what the situation really is. You'd think with women's liberation that it is obvious women want to be independent, but they don't realize not everyone's married with children.'

> 'The general attitude is I'm all right Jack. Most people don't think it'll happen to them. People who have homes and haven't been through it look down on you.'

> 'My parents think I haven't tried. That it's my fault, that it's disgusting.'

Alternatively:

> 'I think there's awful sympathy – people feel sorry for you. They think you're from the moon.'

> 'Some say it's their own fault – others are sympathetic – but they probably wouldn't do anything about it.'

> 'I think the homeless are regarded as victims of circumstance in London – people know the situation's bad. I think it carries more stigma elsewhere.'

> 'Most of my friends are in the same situation, so they

understand. My parents worry about it.'

'My family want me to think of their place as my home.'

Conclusion

These concepts of homelessness and the women's self-perceptions which derive from them have significant and serious implications. Many women expressed a feeling of inadequacy and failure, they internalized society's blame:

'In most cases it makes people feel they're failures. It becomes difficult to pull yourself up and make the effort. You tend to let yourself go. You feel as if everyone knows you've got nowhere to go.'

Only a small minority expressed anger at the inequity of the system, and the label attached to being homeless:

'There's so little said about the difficulties single people experience in struggling to get a place. Single people are considered secondary, they don't matter. Everyone expects you to go and live at home with your parents. So that's what you go and do.'

Thus for many women, being homeless or in housing need implied powerlessness, insecurity and self-reproach.

Closely related to this point is the fact that 42 per cent of women interviewed did not define themselves as homeless, despite either living in a hostel or having contacted a housing advice agency for homeless people. This was because they did not fit their own definition of homeless. Yet the accepted image or notion of homelessness which many of these women have in mind – 'little old men with bags on their shoes', almost inevitably excludes women. This is a crucial point, since if homeless women do not define themselves as homeless, who will?

This leads to an important conclusion. The more that people in housing need, or homeless people, do not recognize their housing need or homelessness, the less they will act to change the situation or challenge the system that confronts them. As one woman explained:

'I think one ought to say one's homeless and then you try and do something about it. I mean until I think of myself as homeless, I won't do anything. I used to think of homelessness as someone on their own on a street corner – and because I had friends, I didn't think of myself as homeless. But in fact I've been homeless for a long time, in that I've never had a place I could call my own. The system makes you have that impression too and that's how it keeps you down and stops you from doing anything. The media has the same idea of homelessness as I used to before I started calling myself homeless. They think it means people like gypsies, and they don't think of people like me. So they make no inroads to doing anything about it.'

The more individuals with housing problems blame themselves for their situation, again, the less likely they are to rebel against it either individually or collectively. It is through such processes that homelessness or housing problems become concealed. It is this lack of collective action which accounts in part for the minimal recognition of single people's housing needs and the consequent lack of provision. Once again, therefore, we see the significance of definitions of homelessness for the nature of housing provision.

CHAPTER 7

Women's housing and homelessness: a focus on the family

How do women lose accommodation and end up in a hostel or with nowhere secure to live? What are the relevant social and economic relationships which structure homeless women's current position at various points along the home-to-homelessness continuum from sleeping rough to security of tenure? Indeed, do homeless women constitute a homogeneous group and is it simply accidental that some women live in hostels while for others their homelessness or housing need is more concealed? Do factors such as mental illness and social relationships, emphasized by many homelessness studies (e.g. DHSS, 1976), have an impact on women's homelessness? These are the issues we set out to explore in the next two chapters looking first at the impact of the family, and second at women's labour market status and its relevance for their housing.

Before analysing the relationships which explain the women's different housing histories and current situation, we need to explore what these differences actually are. First, a similar proportion of the concealed homeless (14 per cent) and up-market hostel women (19 per cent) became homeless after losing owner-occupied accommodation, whereas very few of the direct-access hostel women and none of the women's aid women had become homeless from this sector. In contrast, many more women from the latter two groups (29 per cent and 82 per cent respectively) had lived in local authority housing immediately before the onset of homelessness.

Housing in the private rented sector had preceded homelessness for the largest number of the concealed homeless group (43 per cent) and for 28 per cent of the direct- access hostel women, with smaller numbers of the other two groups becoming homeless from this sector. If we investigate the women's housing histories we find that for approximately a quarter of these women from direct-access hostels, friends, relatives, sublets and shortholds had been their only (relatively) secure or long-stay housing during their adult lives. Tied accommodation signifies as an important source of housing for the concealed homeless and the direct-access hostel women. The overall housing histories of the women reveal a similarity between the direct-access hostel and women's aid women on the one hand, and the concealed homeless and the up-market hostel women on the other, in relation to the two major tenures. An overwhelming majority of the women from the women's aid centres and 37 per cent of the direct-access hostel women had lived in local authority housing at some point. In contrast, no women from the up-market hostels and only a few of the concealed homeless women had been accommodated in this sector. The picture for owner-occupation is the exact reverse. No women from refuges, and only 10 per cent of the direct-access hostels women had lived in this sector, whereas approximately one-third of the other two groups had lived in owner-occupied property as adults.

Further, private rented accommodation was a more significant element in the overall housing experiences of the concealed homeless women than it was for others. Women in the concealed group do not appear to use hostels as a solution to their housing problems: only 12 per cent had ever stayed in hostels. On the other hand once a woman had lived in a hostel, if she found rehousing from there which she subsequently had to leave she frequently returned to a hostel: 73 per cent of the women in direct-access hostels had lived in more than one hostel.

Differences are also apparent in the length of time that the women had been homeless. In this respect, the greatest similarities are between the concealed homeless women and the women's aid women, the majority of whom had been homeless for less than one year. In the case of the women's aid women this reflects the active rehousing policies of the workers in the women's aid centres, which are discussed later. For the concealed homeless women, it is not possible to draw any substantive conclusions except to say that the concealed homeless women interviewed tended to have approached the advice centre about their housing problems a short time after their onset.

In contrast over half the direct-access and up-market hostel women had been homeless for over a year with as many as 57 per cent of the latter group having been homeless for more than three years.

Marriage

Given the centrality of the nuclear family to housing access, we would expect the women who had married or cohabited to have had different experiences and faced different problems in the housing market from the women who had never married or cohabited. The qualitative and the quantitative data supports this hypothesis.

We have argued that women's access to secure housing in the public and owner-occupied sectors is dependent in the former case on being a mother first and foremost, and a wife, and in the latter case on being appended to a male wage or salary earner. We would expect, therefore, a larger proportion of the women who had been married and had had children to have lived in one of these two sectors at some juncture in their lives. This indeed was the case: 36 per cent of ever-married women compared with 8 per cent of never-married women had lived in local authority housing, with similar figures – 25 per cent compared to 4 per cent for owner-occupation. Similarly, many more of the married women had become homeless from these sectors and had subsequently been unable to find adequate alternatives. What then are the processes through which women lost access to the marital home?

Reasons for loss of accommodation

The common mythology is that women tend to be granted, or remain in, the marital home on marital breakdown while their partners are obliged to leave. This assumption derives from a focus on marital breakdown where dependent children are involved. It is indeed usual practice for the courts to grant owner-occupied property to the custodial parent. However this decision may only apply for the duration of the children's dependency, after which time the property is sold and the equity shared. Similarly, local authorities tend to allocate tenancies to the

110

individual who has custody of the children, usually the woman, but this is purely and simply on the basis of her role as a mother[1]. For women without dependents the situation is quite . different. Over one-third of the women interviewed lost housing due to marital dispute.

Research into divorce patterns reveals that women respond to marital problems before men, tending to leave first or take action to change the situation. In 1980, 71 per cent of divorces were petitioned by the female partner (CSO, 1; Table 2.13). Moreover research suggests that men's needs are more easily satisfied by marriage while women have to make greater adjustments in order to make the marriage succeed (Gavin, *et al.*, 1960). This pattern was supported by the study. It showed that 46 per cent of the ever-married had husbands/boyfriends who had remained in the marital home, whereas they had decided to leave when the situation became intolerable. Only 19 per cent had actually been forced to leave; more frequently the women were sure that the situation they had found unbearable would have continued unchanged:

> 'He used to invite other women back, but always said he wanted me to stay too. I did do his cooking and washing after all. But it was clear to me that the marriage had ended, one of us had to go. He wouldn't leave so I had to. I got a job in Blackpool waitressing for the summer, and then I moved into another girl's flat.'

Another woman explained the loss of her sole tenancy where she had latterly lived with her husband:

> 'I thought that I would be able to find somewhere else, since I had never had any trouble with housing before. My husband said he would contest the divorce if I didn't let him have the flat, and I couldn't face a long drawn out case with all our marital problems aired publicly, so I left. Peabody transferred the flat into his name and refused to offer me anywhere. I would never have left had I realised what would happen.'

Lack of knowledge of the housing system and a refusal to live with someone where the relationship had broken down had left this woman homeless.

Other women were forced to go either quite openly by their husbands or because of insufficient claim to the housing tenure on their own behalf. Women spoke of giving up their own housing on marriage to accommodate their lives to the needs and desires of their husband:

'I had my own secure unfurnished flat which I gave up to go and live with my boyfriend in his flat. I went to look after him. He was that type. I did the housekeeping and secretarial work. The place had all his things in it and his daughter was there a lot. His choice. It was my home but I didn't have a choice over who came and went. He started another relationship, so I moved out. He didn't want me to move out, I was very reliable and doing lots of things for him. By then, of course, I had no flat left to go to.'

An important way that women accommodated their husband's needs focused on the men's employment. The ideological acceptance of the primacy of men's work shone through in many women's comments. Two trends were most marked. One was where the men's employment took the couple abroad. When the marital relationship ended through death or divorce, many women's inclination was to return to England with the notion of England as their 'home'. The irony was that their age, lack of resources and contacts after many years' absence meant that the possibility of finding accommodation was if not non-existent, at best slender. Yet, to stay abroad once the marriage had ended was frequently not an option either. Social life may have been centred around the man's work, leaving the woman on her own, isolated and lonely. Her lack of financial resources, or employment prospects may also have influenced her departure, or the housing she had lived in may have been tied to her husband's employment. Whatever the reason, a woman returning to London after many years away finds herself extremely disadvantaged in the housing market.

One woman described having lived in Kenya for twenty-three years with her husband in services' accommodation; he began to have affairs and the marriage deteriorated:

'I got the boot, I was packed on the aeroplane like a brown paper parcel and sent home.[2] I assumed I'd be able to find somewhere or stay with my brother, but all I found was a hostel.'

Women returning from abroad often rely on their children for a roof for many months, sometimes causing great domestic strain in an already overcrowded household.

The problems associated with living in accommodation tied to a spouse's employment were not restricted to women who had lived abroad. Five women had become homeless on marital breakdown because they had no rights to the husband's tied accommodation. None of the women were reallocated the tenancy in their own right – instead the dependence on an ex-husband's 'goodwill' was reinforced. As an ex-wife of a policeman explained:

'My husband walked out four months after we got married, but I was told that as long as he was still in the police force and we stayed married it was all right for me to stay there. But he left the force in January, so I was given notice to quit.'

It is clear that the tendency for women to accommodate themselves to their husband's lives thereby minimizes their own access to housing. The third point in relation to marital breakdown is the structural inequality within the marital or cohabiting relationship and more generally within the household. The household cannot be seen as a cohesive unit within which each member's relation to the housing tenure is equal or where the financial resources of one member are necessarily shared. The household exists within a patriarchal and capitalist society where some individuals have more resources and power than others. The implications for homeless women's access (specifically homeless women who have been married) to housing are clear.

Conventionally in tax and related matters, the household is treated as one unit where individual interests are aggregated, the assumption being that benefits and assets are distributed. Thus, a married working man is granted a tax allowance on the assumption that he will support his family. Similarly mortgage tax relief accrues to the mortgagor within the household, often the man, on the assumption that the whole household will

113

benefit. However it is one person, most frequently the male 'head of household' who benefits directly; the extent to which he redistributes these gains amongst other household members is his decision. Studies have shown that married women not only lack their own income, particularly during the early child-rearing years, but they lack control over their husband's income (Pahl, 1980), that a rise in male wages is not automatically accompanied by a rise in women's housekeeping allowances (Young, 1952, p. 15), that some wives are kept in ignorance of their husband's earnings (Gover, 1971) and that in some cases men keep their wages for their own use leaving the wife to manage the housekeeping on her own income (Jephcott and Smith, 1962). For women who have little economic independence or control of financial resources within the marriage, the problems associated with leaving and setting up independently are inevitably exacerbated.

The structural inequality between men and women, and men's power within the household has different implications in the public and private housing sectors. We argued earlier that the traditional notion of men providing shelter for the family formerly meant that more sole council tenancies were granted to married men than married women, and referred to the fact that this practice has changed. This was supported by the women interviewed. Of the seventeen women who had lived with their husbands in council accommodation in the years preceding the woman's last two housing situations, there were seven joint tenancies, and ten circumstances where the husband was the sole tenant. In contrast, where the woman's most recent accommodation was in the public sector in only two cases did the man hold the tenancy alone.

The more recent local authority practice of granting joint tenancies to both partners has brought its own problems. Before the 1980 Housing Act council tenants had no security of tenure. This meant that in cases of marital breakdown, particularly where there was domestic violence, a local authority could evict the male partner transferring the joint tenancy to a sole one for the woman, or in the case of sole tenancies in the man's name, transferring his right to the tenancy and reallocating this tenancy, or a new one, to the woman. Although security of tenure for council tenants clearly represents a progressive step, where a marital relationship breaks down and both partners are joint tenants, serious housing problems can ensue. The major problem which women's campaigning groups have raised is the difficulty of evicting the male tenant, especially in cases of domestic violence. Frequently local authorities advise women to return home with a court injunction to restrain their husbands although such injunctions are notoriously ineffective. Where no children are involved local authorities are even less likely to rehouse the woman when a relationship ends. With the reduction in the housing stock and less and less possibility of transfers to alternative accommodation, women are increasingly advised to stay where they are.

After living in local authority housing all her life as a joint tenant with her husband Caroline decided to leave:

'The marriage had become unbearable. I'd had enough, he'd had women all along – even a child by one, and he'd started to threaten and frighten me.'

Unfortunately her youngest child was twenty-one years old, so in the council's terms she had no dependents and was thus refused rehousing.

'The only reason I stayed in the marriage so long was because I was adopted and I think the family is important – children need that. Yet people tell me I should have left before and then I would have got rehoused, ridiculous isn't it? You're on the rubbish heap once you're my age. Now I've brought up the kids and they're grown up, no one cares. And they treat my son like that too – they say he can go and lodge some place, just because he hasn't got a family. Neither of us are thought to be entitled to a home, yet I always paid my rent, kept the flat nice, I've never been in arrears and I've lived round here all my life. They tell me I still have a tenancy and to go back there. But how can I be expected to live with him, his new woman and her kids?'

Not only does this situation illuminate the problems that can ensue from joint tenancies under the 1980 Act; it also illustrates the expectation that women should depend on their husbands for housing and devote their lives to their children. This was a recurrent theme, many women moving to live close to their children when they needed support, and thereby losing the limited housing rights they had.

The increase in owner-occupation makes the question of how women without dependents can keep or obtain alternative owner-occupied accommodation an important one. Of the twenty-six women who had lived in owner-occupied property during their marriage, in seventeen cases the man was the sole mortgagor, one woman had a sole mortgage, and eight mortgages were joint. Since the Matrimonial Homes Act 1967 women have been able to negotiate for a property settlement through a solicitor or through the courts, regardless of which partner held the mortgage. Nevertheless, several women had left the marital home both before and after the Act without gaining any financial share.

The Matrimonial Homes Act 1967 sets out the rights of the two partners to the matrimonial home. If a woman wants to remain in the home there are several options she can take (see Leevers and Thynne, 1979). She can have the mortgage transferred into her name in exchange for reduced, or no maintenance. She can have the property transferred to her name and then raise the money to pay her husband his share, or decide to stay until the youngest child leaves school. The problem with all these solutions is ultimately financial. If a woman has a low income or no income at all the difficulties of paying the mortgage or paying her husband his share may be too difficult to surmount. On the other hand, agreeing to take a share in the equity and leaving the home entails other problems. If the woman wants to re-enter the owner-occupied sector she will need to persuade a building society to grant her a mortgage which will be difficult if she is on a low income and her employment prospects after many years out of the labour market are poor. The older she is the greater the problems she will face.

For women who have been cohabiting with their partner and who are not legally married, the situation is exacerbated. If the home is owned jointly the woman is entitled to her share. However, if the property is solely owned in the man's name, her rights are severely limited. When the couple are married the woman is usually entitled to one-third of the equity if the house is in the man's name – this rule does not apply to cohabitees – yet, even when women gain a lump sum payment, they find it gradually whittled away as they support themselves in the private-rented sector, as the only option. Clearly, where no dependents are involved, and a relationship breaks down, the housing outcome for women who were living in owner-occupied property is a complex one.

One interviewee, in her thirties, was in the process of separating from her husband and the proceeds of the house sale were due to be shared equally. Her husband was able to move to a similar sized house, but she was forced to take a drop in her material standard of living; her wages, £3,600 per annum, as a sales clerk, being too low to enable her to obtain or pay a large mortgage:

> 'I have bought a new one-bedroomed house on a mortgage with a young girl from work. The building society wouldn't give me a mortgage on my own, so I had to get her to join in, though I'd rather get a place on my own. It means we shall have a bedsit each and a shared kitchen. I would have preferred a council tenancy, I don't want a mortgage hanging round my neck, but it was the last resort.'

Her husband, in contrast, did not see his mortgage as a burden. This is an interesting example of hidden structural inequality within a household which was only unmasked when the household unit broke down.

Related to the financial problems associated with marital breakdown is the situation where a woman's husband dies and she cannot afford to remain in the dwelling. Ten women had lost secure housing in this way. Some found the mortgage repayments too high while others found the on-going cost of maintenance and repair of the property beyond their means. Frequently these women mentioned that their dependence on husbands for their housing had only become clear when the support was withdrawn or lost.

Second, interviewing the homeless women it was clear that the ideological force of the notion of men's employment as primary had significant implications for women's housing in the owner-occupied sector:

> 'Our house was worth £50,000. The marriage broke and I left because he wasn't going to. I wanted to come back to

117

London, I didn't like Andover, but we'd moved there for his work. There was no property settlement as we're not legally separated. When I left I was taking my freedom, so I decided I wouldn't take anything. The house is the epitome of all that he's worked for, it means a lot more to him than to me so I can't take it away from him.'

Finally, in the rare instances (10 per cent of cases) where men gain custody of the children, women have to leave the marital home and find housing. If the couple were living in owner-occupied property, legal property settlements are unlikely to be very favourable to the woman, particularly if the property was owned by the man; frequently the agreement is merely an informal one, and solicitors are not involved:

'I literally left home one night with two suitcases and nowhere to go. It was very frightening. I was cushioned though because I had some money and knew I could book into a hotel – unlike some women. We decided he should stay in the house because he was keeping my son. I wasn't given any money or anything. He couldn't afford to buy me out as it was a joint mortgage. I rang up some flat-sharers, one woman said she couldn't bear to share with someone who'd left a child.'

Children

Thirty-eight per cent of the women had had children at some stage in their lives, although by definition these children were no longer dependent on their mothers. Women's aid women were the most likely to have children who were of a dependent age but were currently separated from their mothers. Similarly, a large proportion of the direct-access hostel women's children were in care, fostered or living with relatives at the time of the inter-view. In contrast the majority of the children of the concealed homeless and up-market hostel women were adults. The fact that more women in the direct-access group had children in care or fostered derives in part from their marginalized economic and social status, which sets them apart from the concealed home-less and up-market hostel women in several important ways. This argument is elaborated later.

There is a strong relationship between women, their children and housing. The most important feature of this relationship is that not only do children constitute a route to housing access, they also constrain women in their access to housing. We described how one woman stayed in an intolerable marriage 'for the sake of her children' – this is not an unusual decision. Similarly women move to live closer to their children when support is needed, even if this jeopardises their own prospects:

'I returned from Africa in 1972 to find my daughter in a state of collapse – her marriage was breaking up. So I moved to Worcestershire to be near her and gave up an offer of permanent housing in London which I had.'

A further issue is custody; the rehousing custody conundrum is well known to those involved with cases of marital breakdown. Standard local authority practice is to refuse to rehouse a woman until she has custody of her children, while at the same time the woman's chances of gaining custody are slim when she has no housing for them. One woman in a women's aid centre described her battle:

'The council won't give me a big enough place until I get custody of the kids. He's still living in the council flat – it was his tenancy – and he wants the kids too. If the welfare from the courts come to look round here it's not very good for the custody case, because it's so crowded. Hackney offered me a place – but I refused it. They said it was the last offer I would get. It was filthy, no heating, a basement flat, plaster falling off the walls, dark and damp. It only had two rooms – no room for the kids. A shared bathroom and toilet. The council said I could put the kids in the sitting-room. It was hopeless. They were trying to dump me off with anything. I would have been really stuck, I knew no one in the area.'

Three lesbian women spoke of an added difficulty – the discrimination they met from the courts and socal services on account of their sexuality. The likelihood of these women successfully obtaining housing and custody was even further removed.

119

Parents

The centrality of the family to housing operates at many levels, the parental family being of specific relevance to single women. Again, there are dual standards of acceptable behaviour for unmarried men and for unmarried women. Many women described the pressure exerted by their parents to live at home, the only legitimate reason for leaving parents being to marry and set up 'a home of one's own'. Thus a woman exchanges dependence on her father for her housing as a young woman, for dependence on another man, her husband, for her accommodation as an adult. Clearly, there are legitimate ways out of this sequence for some women, through moving to college, finding employment or simply getting established on their own or with friends, but the housing options are limited and the social pressures to remain within the 'bosom of the family' are strong.

The parental family was thus an important source of housing, intermittently or for many years, for some of the women who had never married. In some cases this represented a positive choice, the parental home being a secure and comfortable base, while for others it simply represented a lack of alternative options. Other women stayed with their parents from time to time as a fall-back, while moving between different housing situations or jobs.

In the second place, there is social and ideological pressure on women to extend their caring role to care for elderly and sick relatives. Decreasing public expenditure on social services combined with an ageing population has caused an increase in the number of women who care for elderly dependents. Three times as many old people live with married daughters as with married sons (Phillipson, 1981, p.189) and 300,000 single women look after an elderly parent. Women who have no dependents of their own are frequently under greater familial and social pressure to perform this caring role, particularly because it is often seen to be easier for a single woman to move to live with her parents, than it is for a woman with her own family. Several women had found themselves in this position.

At the time of both the parent(s) death single women, who have been living in the parental home, are likely to encounter housing problems. Among the women interviewed ten had lost secure housing on the death of their parents. In the public sector before the 1980 Housing Act (S, p.30, 32, 34) which gave security of tenure to council tenants, and right of succession to their children, children of council tenants could not automatically take over their parents' tenancy when the parents died. Local authorities tended to operate *ad hoc* policies in this event. One woman had lived with her mother for fifteen years in a council flat in her mother's name. One year after she died the council demolished the flats. The council refused to rehouse the daughter, although they informed her that a male member of the household would have qualified for rehousing. Since then she had moved between bed and breakfast hotels and hostels; she was unable to find a bedsit with an affordable rent or where a deposit was not required. She was unaware that her low income entitled her to a rent allowance had she been able to find somewhere.

Several women had lived with parents in owner-occupied property and likewise had lost their housing when their parents had died. Two of these women had gone to live with their parents latterly in order to look after them in their old age. The parents of these and several other women had left their house to be shared equally among the children. In each case the woman's share of the equity was not sufficient to enable her to purchase any property outright, and the usual difficulties of obtaining a mortgage applied. For other women the loss of a secure housing base with their parents was traumatic at an emotional as well as material level.

For women remaining in the parental home as an adult through lack of alternatives there are different problems, which are related to the secondary status that single people within the family often have:

> 'If my married sisters and brothers come to stay, I end up on the sofa as I'm the single one, and they have my bedroom . . . I have no privacy, mother won't let me shut the bathroom door even.'

Nine women had been forced to leave the parental home because of domestic disputes which had made living together intolerable. A further nine said that their family had put pressure on them to return home when their marriage broke down considering them incapable of fending for themselves without the support of a man.

It is clear from this evidence that the nuclear family in its different forms underlies access to housing for many women. It is also clear that the demise of the family structure, be it marital breakdown or death of parents can often mean homelessness for the women involved. To what extent, therefore, can marital/ family dispute or death in the family account for the differences between the four homeless groups? It would appear from our data that marital breakdown does not in itself account for the differences in housing experiences between the concealed home- less and direct-access women referred to earlier since a similar proportion (36 per cent and 33 per cent respectively) of these two groups lost secure accommodation following marital breakdown. There were also no significant differences in the incidence of family dispute between the direct-access hostel and concealed homeless women which account for the differences in housing histories. In contrast only a small number of the up-market hostel group lost accommodation due to marital/family dispute, reflecting the admission policies of these hostels which favour never-married working women on a non-emergency basis. Finally, death of a spouse caused the loss of accommodation for similar numbers of concealed homeless (8 per cent), direct-access hostel (5 per cent) and up-market hostel (10 per cent) women[3]. Thus, although these factors explain some of the differences between the housing histories of ever-married and never- married women and represent important reasons for homeless- ness, they do not account for the housing differences between groups. Before considering other possible explanations for these we examine the housing experiences of the never-married women, and the married women in their single status, since it is obviously not the case that the only route to secure housing is through family membership, although it is an important one.

The housing histories of single women

Only four women who had never married or cohabited had ever lived in owner-occupied property, and only eight of the never- married women had lived in local authority accommodation, five of whom had gained access to this sector through their status as mothers, leaving three who had been granted their own tenancies as women without dependants. The two major forms of housing tenure in Britain are clearly not accessible to many single women. How then do women on their own house themselves? Obviously there is not one answer; there are as many solutions as the women interviewed, and as many different strategies adopted to solve their housing problems. However, a range of housing patterns does emerge from the interviews.

With the recent sharp decrease in the private rented sector, it is not surprising to find that only a small proportion of women had been tenants in this sector in more recent years. However, in 24 per cent of cases the women's last secure accommodation – which many women had left some years previously – was in the private rented sector. The reasons for loss of private rented accommodation are: eviction, both legal and illegal, a request to leave, and a tenant's decision to leave. Evictions are by no means the major cause of loss of private-rented housing. In 26 per cent of cases women left private rented housing on request from their landlord, because the landlord wanted to repossess the premises for his own purposes. In many cases the women had protected tenancies but were not interested in, or prepared to fight for, their right to remain. The following response illuminates one reason why:

> 'The council say that I should get a court order to stay here, but he has been a very good landlord, so I didn't want to sue him. He hasn't given me any bother so why should I give him any?'

Some women were unaware of their rights, while others left because the accommodation did not suit their needs. Similar numbers of women moved because the flat had become too expensive, their income had dropped, the physical conditions were intolerable or detrimental to their health, they had rent arrears, or were in dispute with their landlord or neighbours. Other women had lost accommodation due to domestic dispute, or had left to take up a new job, or training, or to look after a relative or friend.

The second major source of housing, and indeed employment, for the single women was tied accommodation. As many as 38 per cent of the total sample and 48 per cent of the women who had never married had lived in tied accommodation at some juncture. With tied accommodation in agriculture – traditionally an area of male employment – often dominating the terms of the debate, it is interesting to see the prevalence of women in this sector.

The link between housing and employment is a significant one, and is explored further in the next chapter. Of relevance here is that women's choice of employment, where tied accommodation was offered, was in many cases a decision to solve a housing problem, not an employment one. This was particularly true for women whose only employment prospects were in the hotel, catering and health service sectors, where low wages militate against the possibility of finding affordable housing in the private sector. A study on tied accommodation endorses this picture: 85 per cent of hotel and catering jobs, and 88 per cent of hospital jobs in the survey were being performed by women (Ramsay, 1979).

Of the 41 per cent of women from direct access hostels who had lived in tied accommodation, one quarter had spent all their adult life moving between hostels and tied accommodation, with no other housing alternative. When women were made redundant from their employment, or were forced to leave for any other reason, hostel accommodation was the only option. Women whose marriages had ended, whose years out of the labour market excluded them from entry into many areas of employment, and whose lack of financial resources placed severe housing constraints on them, entered the tied service sector as a last and only resort.

For some of the concealed homeless women who were in tied accommodation at the time of the interview, the arduous nature, and consequent ill-health effects of much of the employment in this sector, meant that had there been any housing alternative available, they would have left their job immediately. One woman, for example, was a caretaker in a students' hostel. Her job entailed walking up and down stairs many times during the day; her legs troubled her, and her health was deteriorating. She was aged fifty-eight years. The local authority would not help her, and she could not bear the thought of living in a hostel. Her only option was to remain in her job.

Age is an important component of the issue for many single

women. Nurses made the point that living in nurses' homes was only tolerable for younger women. They had found, as they became older, the strain of living with women who were mostly much younger than themselves in a student hostel atmosphere difficult to tolerate. This, combined with the expectation of better housing that age brought, the expansion of their own housing needs, and the frustration of many years of institutional living, made life for many residential nurses intolerable:

> 'It's okay sharing when you're young. Now I wish I hadn't come in to nursing – because I've got stuck in this situation. I wouldn't mind doing something different – but where can I leave to? I have somewhere, but it's hampering my life. I can't go in the bathroom or kitchen without always finding someone in there.'

Another problem that women mentioned was the seasonal nature of tied employment, particularly in the hotel and catering sector which inevitably leads to a life of insecurity and constant mobility.

Living in tied accommodation, because no viable alternative exists, is one way a woman's housing need or homelessness is concealed. Another is through the most insecure housing option of all, that is, staying with friends, relatives, on other peoples' floors, and in sublets. Forty-three per cent of the concealed homeless were interviewed in such a situation, with a similar proportion having lived with friends or relatives immediately before their current situation. Friends were significant in the housing histories of all the women, although to a lesser extent in the other three groups. Many women spoke of housing themselves in this manner for several or more years and for 21 per cent of the total sample, staying with friends had constituted the only housing situation they had remained in for any length of time. Furthermore, for 35 per cent of the women, this insecure form of housing tenure was the only housing in their adult life that they had considered to be their 'home'. The fact that women continue to move through such unsatisfactory and dependent housing situations clearly derives from the lack of alternative provision. Many of the concealed homeless women considered the prospect of hostel living to be an anathema, with the result that their homelessness remained concealed. But, for the women in hostels who had been socially isolated for many years, such an option obviously did not exist. Clearly, such accommodation is inherently insecure since the woman is dependent on the tenant or owner's goodwill, and as soon as there is a change of circumstances or a dispute, she can be asked to leave, with no housing rights to protect her.

Although we have explored the processes by which women become homeless or lose secure accommodation, we have not explained the differences in housing histories between the women in terms of the prevalence of one tenure over the other in specific sample groups. It is to an analysis of factors which may affect women's housing experiences that we now turn.

The importance of social and psychological factors

Chapter 6 referred to the high incidence of mental illness or history among the homeless which other studies have emphasized. The incidence of mental illness in this research was far higher in the direct-access hostel group (32 per cent – a figure similar to that reported in the DHSS (1976) study) than in the concealed homeless group (3 per cent) or up-market hostel group (unreported). The connection between mental illness and homelessness is stronger for the direct-access hostel women, since moving from hospital to hostel is frequently the only possibility, as the policy of discharging psychiatric patients into the community is not adequately supported by suitable housing resources. A similar relation between drink problems and housing insecurity is also revealed. Of the fourteen women who spoke of having 'problems with drink' either currently or previously, none had ever lived in owner-occupied property, only one had had a secure tenancy in the private rented sector, and half had lived in the local authority sector.

The data can, however, be interpreted in several ways with varying implications. Mental illness/alcohol problems could be seen as one consequence of institutionalized and insecure hostel living. On the other hand it can be argued that women who have had psychiatric problems are likely to end up in hostels because they are unable to cope on their own or secure their own housing. Or a third argument might be that women discharged from mental hospitals, who lack material resources or social networks are likely to approach hostels through necessity. In our view the incidence of mental illness (and alcohol problems) is merely one factor which predisposes an individual to institutionalized homelessness for a variety of material, social and psychological reasons, and that emphasis on mental illness/alcoholism as a dominant aspect of institutionalized homelessness is misconceived.

It has also been argued (Batten, 1969, appendix) that homelessness, in particular institutionalized homelessness, is closely associated with a history of broken homes in childhood. This argument supports the pathological and individual model of welfare which was discussed earlier. The idea behind this argument is that children from 'broken homes' or non-traditional two-parent headed nuclear families, are socially or psychologically hampered in their attempts to establish their own conventional household and income. Again, it is a question of how the data is theoretically interpreted. In this study one striking difference emerged between women who were brought up in conventional families and women who were not. Of the twenty-nine women who had ever lived in owner-occupied property during their adult life, only one woman had been brought up in a non-traditional household. Instead, tied accommodation and local authority accommodation was of greater significance in the housing histories of the women from the non-traditional family backgrounds. Since eighteen of the twenty-four women who were not brought up in a two-parent headed family currently lived in direct-access hostels it would appear that there was some connection between 'non-traditional family' upbringing and being homeless in an institutional sense. However, this pattern of moving through a range of insecure housing options or relying on the public sector, could be theorized with different emphases. We consider that the emphasis should be placed on the lack of material and financial resources which might be associated with an upbringing by one parent, foster parents or in a children's home, where there is often little opportunity to stay on in higher or further education and little material back-up, and that this perspective is more valid than the limited focus on social or psychological factors.

Third, the data on friendship networks revealed that women who are more socially isolated have less access to the private

127

sector and a greater reliance on the public sector and hostels than women who have more friends and social contact, a greater proportion of whom had lived in the private rented sector or stayed with friends. Finally, although we argued that marital dispute did not explain the differences in housing histories between the four groups of women, the disparity in the incidence of marriage and cohabitation between groups could be significant for other reasons. There are several implications of the fact that women's access to secure housing may often be through dependence on a male partner in marriage. These might include women's lack of knowledge of the housing system, social isolation in the sense of lack of independent friendship networks, and most of all disengagement with the process of finding housing on their own behalf. If at some point after the relationship has broken down the accommodation is lost, married women are likely to be less equipped to obtain adequate rehousing than women who have had to fend for themselves in a competitive and limited (for single people) housing market. In this instance, direct-access hostels are one of the few available options. Related to this point is that marriage for some women, particularly those who marry young, may imply a withdrawal from the educational/training process in order to take up an expected role within the home as housewife and mother.

Similarly, it is likely that the fact that more direct-access hostel women (than concealed homeless women) had had children at some juncture is significant, since childcare responsibilities affect women's labour force participation (DE and OPCS, 1983) which in turn may affect these women's access to housing in the private sector. This inter-relationship between women's domestic role and their position in the labour market is a crucial part of the sexual division of labour which is central to an understanding of women's access to housing. This theme is developed in the chapter which follows.

CHAPTER 8

Homeless women and the labour market

To what extent does a woman's position in the labour market account for her marginalized status in the housing market? Female participation in the UK labour market has distinctive characteristics. Sixty-five per cent of women between sixteen and fifty-nine are in the labour force, although a sizeable proportion of women work part-time, particularly married working women. Women least likely to be in paid employment are those with children under the age of five of whom only 27 per cent are in employment nationally, reflecting women's traditional primary responsibility for childcare and the lack of adequate preschool childcare provision. Second, women are concentrated in particular occupations and industries – clerical work, the service sector and manufacturing, particularly in textiles and light industry, and are under-represented in professional and managerial occupations. Many areas of female employment are characterized by poor working conditions, a low level of unionization and low pay.

There is a wide discrepancy between average gross hourly earnings for female and male employees. In 1981 women's gross hourly earnings were 241.2 pence per hour compared with 322.5 pence per hour for men. If overtime is taken into consideration, average weekly earnings of women in full-time work per hour fall from 74 per cent to 63 per cent of men's earnings (New Earnings Survey, 1983). This derives from the overtime hours that 58 per cent of men work but from which women are largely excluded on account of their domestic responsibilties. Where women are in better paid employment they tend to be concentrated in the lowest grades even where they are the majority of the workforce. For example, 59 per cent of primary and secon-

129

dary school teachers are women, whereas only 38 per cent of head teachers are female (NUT/EOC, 1980). Women's jobs are frequently defined as less skilled than men's jobs, and women are often excluded from entering the traditionally skilled jobs, either through lack of training or qualifications, or through prejudice and ideological pressures to remain in traditionally female areas of employment. These sexual inequalities remain despite the passing of the Equal Pay Act which came into force in 1975 and the Sex Discrimination Act passed in the same year.

A useful theoretical approach for understanding the inferior economic status of women and homeless women in particular is Marxist-feminist theory, which attempts to understand women's employment position by incorporating an analysis of family structure and the ideology of female domestic responsibility (see Bruegel, 1983; Beechey, 1978). Labour market processes and the division of labour within the family appear to reinforce one another. Women's responsibilities as wife and mother lead them to take part-time work which can be organized around these. Likewise their caring role in the home leads to an ideological construction that suitable work for women is in the servicing and caring sectors. The assumption of female financial dependence on a male partner and the notion of a female income providing 'extra' or 'pin' money also militate against equal opportunities in the employment sphere. The importance of these issues is recognized and incorporated within a Marxist-feminist analysis.

Homeless women's employment

This section addresses three questions: the similarity or dissimilarity between the employment and education status of homeless women and of the female population at large; the nature of the difference in employment and education status between the four groups of homeless women, and the effects of marital status, age, race and homelessness itself on employment and education status.

In the concealed homeless group, 75 per cent of the women were employed at the time of interview compared with 11 per cent from direct access hostels, 85 per cent from the up-market hostels and only 18 per cent from the women's aid centres. A comparison with the national statistics on economic activity reveals that a higher proportion of the up-market hostel and concealed homeless groups were employed than in the national sample of single, widowed, divorced and separated women. The fact that the lower age limit of the homeless women sample was twenty-five years, and no students were interviewed, might explain this discrepancy. In contrast, far fewer women in the other two groups were employed than women nationally (DE and OPCS 1983).

Since a majority of women were employed at the time of the interview an analysis of the women's last jobs gives a more comprehensive picture of the occupational structure of the homeless women's employment. More concealed homeless women (41 per cent) had recently been engaged in clerical work than in the female workforce nationally (31 per cent); they were also over-represented in professional and managerial occupations. Fewer of these women had recently been employed in catering and cleaning work. The occupational structure of the up-market hostel group exhibits a similar pattern, although an even larger proportion (48 per cent) of these women were engaged in clerical work. This factor, and the low level of current unemployment amongst this group, reflects the tendency of up-market hostels to favour white collar and skilled workers. In contrast, in the direct-access hostels a much larger proportion of women (53 per cent) had worked in the cleaning and catering services industries than in the national female population (32 per cent), while fewer had been employed in the clerical sector. Of the currently employed, the concealed homeless women and the up-market hostel women earned more than the women in the other two groups (Table 8.1). Taking into account a standard single person's tax rate, a comparison with national female average gross weekly earnings of £91.4 for the same year (New Earnings Survey, 1981), which would thus approximate £65.70 a week net, revealed that the majority of the women interviewed earned less than the national female average, and substantially less than the average gross male weekly wage of £140.5. The wages of the direct-access hostel women were particularly low, with only one of the eight women in employment taking home more than £60 a week. Only 26 per cent of the concealed homeless women and 38 per cent of the up-market hostel women earned more than £70 net a week.

Table 8.1 Source of income and net earnings distribution for those working (including overtime pay)

	State benefit %	No income %	(£'s) 21–40 %	41–60 %	61–70 %	71–80 %	80–100 %	100+ %
Concealed Homeless	11 10	3 5	4 7	13 22	11 19	9 14	6 10	1 2
Direct-access hostel group	62 89	– –	3 4	4 6	1 1	– –	– –	– –
Up-market hostel group	3 14	2 10	– –	5 24	3 15	1 4	5 24	2 10
Women's Aid group	8 73	1 9	– –	2 17	– –	– –	– –	– –

Unlike many employed women, the women interviewed had to cover all their own housing costs, which in hostels tend to be very high; it is clear that many of the women would have had difficulty making ends meet. As one dental assistant explained: 'I can't even afford to save for a new pair of shoes or new clothes on that amount (£48 per week after tax). My rent's over £20 before heating costs. I have to miss lunch altogether.' Older women who had become homeless through marital breakdown were particularly vulnerable. As one woman of forty-seven said: 'I feel so lucky to have a job after all those years of being a housewife'. She earned £47 a week for a 40-hour week as a messenger. Interestingly similar numbers of concealed home-less women (41 per cent) to women in the workforce nationally, were in trade unions, whereas only 11 per cent of all the hostel women were trade union members.

The groups also differed in their reasons for leaving their last jobs and their periods of unemployment. The main reason given by the concealed homeless for leaving their last job was to take up a new one (22 per cent). A further 18 per cent left because the employment had been temporary and had come to an end, 8 per cent said they did not like the job, 8 per cent were made redundant and 8 per cent left due to illness. A similar pattern emerged from the up-market hostel interviews. Once again, the picture was entirely different for the direct-access hostel women and the women from refuges: 26 per cent of the women in direct-access hostels left their last employment because of illness, 13 per cent were made redundant, 13 per cent did not like the job, 12 per cent left temporary employment and 9 per cent were sacked. Very few of these women left their job for the 'positive' reason of taking up a new job. In the women's aid group, 27 per cent had left their last job because they disliked it, and a further 27 per cent left because of troubles at home or pregnancy. In a national survey (DE and OPCS, 1983) the main non-domestic reason for leaving the last job given by the unemployed was not liking the job, with illness given as the most important cause of job loss by all non-working women who had worked at some point. In this instance, there appear to be parallels between the direct-access group and all non-working women nationally.

Information on the intentions of the unemployed is always difficult to evaluate. Social pressure to be in employment might make people say they are looking for paid work when they are not. The unemployed women were asked if they had applied for jobs during their period of unemployment, and an overwhelming majority (75 per cent) replied affirmatively, with more concealed homeless women (88 per cent) having applied for jobs than women from the direct-access hostels. The period of unemployment of this latter group also tended to be longer. The recession appears to have affected women in hostels particularly badly, since the catering jobs that were easily found in periods of near-to-full employment, were now being taken by women who were younger and seen as more employable. Naturally women felt badly about this:

'I hate to be idle. I'd do any general work, domestic work, laundry work, hotel work, but all I've heard of is a couple of hours cleaning going. That's no good. You apply for jobs and they tell you they've had masses of applications and they'll let you know, but they never do. They give the jobs to young girls.'

An analysis of the homeless women's changing employment position since the time they lost their last secure accommodation is particularly interesting. With the exception of the women from refuges, a similar proportion of each group (approximately

60 per cent) were employed to the percentage of women employed nationally in 1980. However, many more women nationally who were not currently employed in 1980, were students (and thus may be able to find employment at a later date) than in the sample of homeless women. Amongst the women interviewed, with the exception of the concealed homeless, more women were economically inactive at the time of losing their last home. Further, a larger number of the concealed homeless women and a far greater proportion of the up-market hostel group were employed in the clerical sector at the time they lost their last secure accommodation than in the national female population. At a similar juncture in their housing history direct-access hostel women were more likely to be employed in catering and cleaning, with a much smaller number in professional occupations and sales jobs than the average female population.

If the shifts in the homeless women's employment status are analysed over time some significant differences are revealed. Evidence from the concealed homeless women suggests some indication of upward mobility. The data on employment after losing their last secure accommodation shows that there was a drop in unemployment of 20 per cent, with the result that more of these women were employed (70 per cent) than the national rate for single women. Also, there was an increase in the number of women in skilled[1] and clerical employment. The direct-access hostel group employment patterns appear to differ substantially. Amongst these women unemployment rises upon loss of secure accommodation from 45 per cent to 69 per cent, far outweighing the national unemployment figure for single women. This employment was mainly lost in the unskilled (catering in particular) sector. The information on the employment of the up-market hostel group reveals greater similarities with the concealed homeless: at the time of losing their last secure accommodation 33 per cent were unemployed, this figure fell to 14 per cent after this point. The main increase in employment for these women also took place in the skilled and clerical sectors. If the time spent in employment over the last five years is compared, we find that the concealed homeless and the up-market hostel women have again been employed for a substantially greater proportion of time (70 per cent for five years) than women in the other two groups. These dissimilarities reflect other differences between the groups of homeless women in education, training and in the incidence of marriage, with implications for employment opportunities, which are discussed below.

Sex discrimination

We wanted to explore women's experiences of sex discrimination. One third of the women, with greater numbers from the concealed homeless and up-market hostel groups, felt that they had been discriminated against on sexual grounds at some point during their working lives. The women mentioned all kinds of discrimination from low pay and lack of promotion to sexual harassment. On lack of promotion one said:

'Yes, yes, I was treated very differently in my last job (in the civil service union). All the management positions except one were occupied by men. Each officer had an assistant – the assistants were all women, the officers all men. Women had to make responsible decisions, but were never seen to make them. There was just no promotion. Moreover, the women always had to run errands, and make the tea and things.'

Several women also mentioned sexual harassment:

'When I came to London I worked in a studio. The boss took a fancy to me. After three months, late one Friday, he sacked me because I didn't want to know. They said they wanted someone younger. I was cracked up. I loved it. I went back in on the Monday and the boss's 18 year old girlfriend was behind the desk.'

Third, women mentioned lack of in-service training possibilities as a form of sex discrimination:

'In my present job [the personnel department for British Gas] you have to prove yourself as a woman. They encourage men to take evening classes and exams. It's the kind of corporation where they think women are okay as secretaries and clerical workers – to get much further you have to prove yourself.'

Why more women in the concealed homeless and up-market hostel groups felt that they had been sexually discriminated against can only be a matter for conjecture. A higher rate of trade union membership amongst the concealed homeless may have been of relevance in their awareness of discrimination; education could also be a contributing element. It is to this that we now turn.

Education and training

It is difficult to compare the education of the homeless women and women nationally since the ages of the women interviewed covered a wide range and thus there is no one appropriate year for comparison. However, the education figures which are most relevant to the largest number of women in the sample – those relating to the early 1960s – show that on average boys were staying on at school until a later age than girls (DES, 1965, Table 3). More men than women were taking advanced courses leading to recognized qualifications at grant-aided establishments between 1954 and 1964 (DES, 1965, Table 10). Also, more men in total were taking non-advanced courses, although in traditionally female subjects, for example Home Economics, women outnumbered men (ibid., Table 14). This discrepancy between men and women is evident at all levels of further education from day release courses to full-time university degrees. It does not simply apply to the 1960s, but is a consistent phenomenon despite relatively equal performance and achievement levels by girls and boys at school. Indeed, the higher or more technical the level of education, the smaller the proportion of female students. Byrne (1978) located this inequality within an analysis of marriage, female dependence and traditional values as to what constitutes 'women's courses' and sex-stereotyping. In her account of state training programmes Wickham (1982) likewise showed how training programmes serve to reinforce existing sexual divisions in and between occupations. This is the context within which homeless women's education and training must also be seen.

There were marked differences between the women. First, the women from direct-access hostels and women's aid centres had left school at a much younger age than the others: 65 per cent

136

and 64 per cent of the former two groups respectively left school at fifteen or younger, compared with 26 per cent of the concealed homeless women and 24 per cent of the up-market hostel women. Second, many more of the concealed homeless and up-market hostel women had been educated at grammar or fee-paying schools than women from the other two groups. Given these discrepancies it is not surprising to find that the concealed homeless and up-market hostel women were more qualified. Only 28 per cent of the former group and 38 per cent of the latter had no school qualifications compared with 77 per cent of the women from the direct-access hostels and 55 per cent of the women's aid women.

Several different reasons were given by the direct access hostel women for leaving school at an early age and for their lack of qualifications. Over half said that there had been no opportunity to continue their education. Other reasons given included family pressures, the necessity of earning an income, pregnancy, the war, lack of confidence and lack of encouragement from the school.

The data on higher or further education reveals similar discrepancies. Eighty-three per cent of the concealed homeless women and all the women from up-market hostels had entered some form of education or training since leaving school, compared with only 39 per cent of the direct access hostel women and 27 per cent of the women from refuges. (This category included all forms of education and training from university and college education to secretarial college, domestic science courses, training on the job, apprenticeships – most commonly hairdressing – and evening courses.) There were notable differences between groups in relation to the type of further education and highest qualifications received. Seventeen per cent of the concealed homeless women's highest qualifications were university or polytechnic degrees, a further 17 per cent were secretarial, business or typing qualifications, 13 per cent were teaching certificates or social work qualifications, 9 per cent were nursing certificates, 8 per cent were other professional qualifications and 3 per cent had received in-service training. Some of these women, particularly the university and polytechnic students, had received further secondary qualifications (including secretarial, teaching, social work, nursing and in-service training).

The highest qualifications of the up-market hostel group showed a similar pattern.

The pattern of qualifications for the other two groups offers a sharp contrast. In the direct-access hostel group, only one woman had obtained a degree, one had obtained a teaching certificate, 9 per cent of women had secretarial or typing qualifications, 3 per cent nursing qualifications and 3 per cent had been trained on the job. The only 2 women from the women's aid centres who had obtained qualifications had secretarial and typing skills. The women were asked whether they wished they had done more training, and not surprisingly, over half of the hostel women replied affirmatively. Many women also said that they would be prepared to undertake training or a course of study if this meant that they could find employment more easily. Most women regretted their lack of training: 'I should have had a better start – better education I mean. That's why I've had to do shopwork. I wouldn't have been so exploited if I'd had a better education.'

Again a wide range of reasons were given for not having entered further or higher education. Some women cited marriage as crucial to their lack of training, or in this case – subsequently wasted training:

'I got married as soon as I finished the secretarial course, so I never used it. Then after 30 years when he died, it was of no use to me. Since then I've done masses of jobs – seasonal work in holiday camps, catering, casual jobs, living-in jobs and periods of unemployment. In the last job I was paid £40 a week with a room.'

Family discouragement, particularly the notion that a girl did not need education since her future role was destined to be a housewife and mother, was another:

'I wanted to be a nurse. I applied and was accepted. My family was furious, they didn't want me to work, so there was a huge row. I threw my papers on the fire and left to do domestic work.'

Some of the older women mentioned the war as having intervened in their education. Others referred to pregnancies, illness or lack of desire on their own part. Several women said that they too had accepted the ideology that women's employment is irrelevant or secondary: 'I'd like more training now [aged thirty-nine]. Women don't think about supporting themselves when they're young and at school'.

To what extent, therefore, do qualifications contribute to the employment status of homeless women? Not surprisingly, if the homeless women with qualifications are compared with the homeless women with no qualifications striking differences do emerge: Many more of the women with qualifications were employed at crucial points in their housing histories, specifically in the professional, skilled and clerical sectors. There was a slight shift amongst qualified women from unemployment and tied health to skilled and clerical work after losing their last secure accommodation. In contrast, although only slightly fewer unqualified women were unemployed at the time of losing their last secure accommodation, by the time of the interview the gap had widened considerably with 65 per cent of this group being unemployed compared with 41 per cent of those with qualifications. A large part of this employment loss is accounted for by loss of jobs in the tied unskilled sector, chambermaid jobs for example, which is a significant employment sector for untrained single women.

Several other important differences are revealed in a comparison of these two groups. Just over half of the qualified homeless women had been employed for four to five of the five years preceding the interview compared with only one-third of those with no qualifications, and of those who were currently employed, two-thirds of the women with qualifications were earning over £60 a week net compared with only a quarter of the working women with no qualifications. Although only a very small number of the employed women were paid overtime, of the ten that were, eight were homeless women with qualifications. Twice as many of the qualified women worked in the public sector where unions tend to be stronger, and pay and conditions better. Indeed, a significantly greater number of the qualified employed women were in trade unions, and awareness of sex discrimination was higher. Finally, more of the qualified women (30 per cent) had left their last job for a 'positive' reason, such as for a new job, or for better pay, than women with no qualification (13 per cent). The overall picture which emerges, therefore, is one where the qualified women tend to have been in the better paid and more organized sectors of employment, and had shorter periods of unemployment.

Marital status, age, race, and homelessness

We suggested in the last chapter that marriage and the process of looking after children and running a family would have implications for women's education and employment. This argument was supported by the women's histories. A consistent theme running through the interviews was the notion that female education and employment had been a secondary concern. Their families, their schools, their potential employers and sometimes the women themselves had assumed that at some point they would marry and depend on a husband for financial support. In the case of women who lived in a social environment where these ideological pressures were strong and where women tended to marry young, we would thus expect a low-level of education and employment. Women who have been married and had children tend to spend at least some years out of the labour market while their children are young, which disadvantages them in employment terms. We were interested, therefore, in the proposition that the homeless women who had been married and who had had children were more likely to be in a weaker employment position than those who had not. A comparison of the two groups does indeed support this contention.

At the point of marital breakdown 56 per cent of the married women were not engaged in any kind of paid employment. This is a substantially higher level of economic inactivity than in the national female married population, where 35 per cent of women are not in paid employment. If employment status at the time of interview of the ever-married and never-married groups are compared, we find that more of the ever-married women were unemployed than the never-married women. Moreover a higher proportion of the never-married women were in skilled or clerical work, with more of the ever-married women working in catering, cleaning and other unskilled work. A further comparison of the two groups reveals that the income of the ever-married women was lower and that these women were less likely to be trade union members than the never-married women (25

140

per cent compared with 37 per cent), and less were aware of sex discrimination at work. This possibly indicates a greater un-awareness of rights at work or a more compliant attitude to-wards work. Finally, it is interesting to compare the economic activity rates of the two groups at the time of losing their last secure accommodation. Forty-seven per cent of the married women were unemployed at the time of losing their last secure accommodation, compared to 34 per cent of the never-married women. Obviously, this had implications for the women's hous-ing prospects which are discussed shortly.

Substantial educational differences between the two groups were also revealed. The married women were almost twice as likely to have left school before the age of sixteen when com-pared with the never-married group. Not surprisingly, there-fore, only 40 per cent of this group obtained qualifications at school, (CSE level or above) while 56 per cent of the never-married women had school qualifications. Likewise, more never-married women (73 per cent) than ever-married women (56 per cent) had entered some form of further training or education (including training on the job or evening courses). When asked if they wished they had done more training, 55 per cent of the married women wished that they had compared with 36 per cent of the other group. The main reasons for their lower educational level were cited as lack of encouragement from their families, pregnancy or marriage. In conclusion then, it appears that the women who had been married were disadvantaged in education and employment terms. Thus the lower employment and educa-tional status of the direct-access hostel and women's aid women can in part be explained by the higher incidence of marriage in each of these groups.

Second, economic activity declines with age. As women get older it becomes more difficult to find employment. This is reflected in the fact that in 1981 nearly half the women aged fifty-five to fifty-nine had been on the unemployment register one year or more compared with one quarter of unemployed women in the twenty to twenty-four age group (OPCS, 1983, p.61). Age did indeed appear to be an important component in the homeless women's employment situation. One fifty-eight-year-old woman had spent six months looking for a job: 'I just haven't been able to find anything – at my age it isn't easy'. She was a trained nursery school teacher. Age also appeared to be a disadvantage for some pension schemes:

'The problem is that most big employers have pension schemes which are a condition of employment. But lots of them you have to join at 50 or around that age. So it's not just a question of thinking I'm too old but the pension problem as well.'

It was not, however, only the older women who mentioned age, many of the younger women did too:

'I would like to work as a mother's help more than anything else, but now I'm 30 I'm too old and unqualified. People either want a young girl straight from school or a qualified nanny. They wouldn't take me and I feel too old to train now.'

Other women mentioned feeling too old for the occupation they were accustomed to: 'I feel too old to be poncing around in a dining-room. It's a young girl's job. I want something more responsible. I want to get into nursing.' Some of the women over retirement age discussed wanting to continue working and being unable to do so, either being compulsorily made to retire, or because the work was beginning to become too arduous. For older women with no adequate housing employment was extremely important:

'I was working in catering at the *Daily Express*. I was made to retire – they don't employ people over 60. I put my age down wrong, so I got away with an extra year. Then someone saw my pension book.'

Given that age affected the women's employment prospects, to what extent did age account for the differences in employment status between the four groups of homeless women? Age was a relevant component. Seventeen per cent of the direct-access hostel women were over sixty at the time of the interview compared with only 7 per cent of the concealed homeless women and no women in the other two groups. A much higher proportion of the concealed homeless and women's aid women were under thirty-five than of the other women. Since the residents at women's aid centres were liable to be unemployed for other reasons (i.e. recent disruption in their lives, marital status, lack of training etc.) we would not expect age to be particularly relevant. However, the fact that more women in the concealed homeless group were younger, could in part have contributed to their higher level of employment when compared to the direct-access hostel group.

The third factor we considered important to explore was race. Despite the lack of systematic records on this issue studies of black women have found that West Indian and Asian women occupy a subordinate position in the labour market. In a study of West Indian women's employment, Phizacklea (1982) found a concentration of West Indian women in the health service, particularly in psychiatric and geriatric hospitals and as trainee nurses; fewer West Indian women were employed in clerical work and as shop assistants than white female workers. Wilson (1978) found many Asian women working in unskilled and lowest paid employment as sweat-shop workers and homeworkers.

The number of West Indian, Asian and African women in the sample of homeless women was small and it is thus difficult to draw any substantial conclusions. Since a similar number of black women were to be found in each group, race cannot account for the employment differences between the groups. Five Asian women, ten West Indian and four African women were interviewed – a total of 12 per cent of the whole sample. There were fewer black women in the up-market hostels than in the other groups which again reflects the relative exclusiveness of this type of provision. A comparison between the black and white women revealed no notable differences in education and employment, except for the fact that there was a greater proportion of nurses among the West Indian group in line with Phizacklea's (1982) findings. Since a higher proportion of the white women in the sample were unemployed or in low paid employment than the national female average, this would account for the lack of significant differences in employment between the black and white homeless women. However, some racial issues concerning employment were raised in the interviews by the black women. For example, discrimination was given by several women as a reason for failing to find employment or for losing jobs. As a forty-year-old unemployed Indian woman explained: 'I was a housekeeper but I left because of the racial prejudice of the other chambermaids'.

Finally, we explored the effect of homelessness or insecure or inadequate housing on the women's employment opportunities. Fifty per cent of the women considered that homelessness had affected their employment prospects. This was in a variety of ways, depending first on the type of employment they sought, and second on the type of accommodation in which they lived. Concern was expressed by the women who had professional or higher status jobs, and those who were self-employed, about the difficulty of keeping clean and dressing well, as is often required in professional employment. As one twenty-nine-year-old business consultant said:

'I wanted to work freelance and have my own individual life
– I can't do that without a proper home. It makes travel
impossible. I have no control. I can't be efficient and smartly
dressed living in a grotty place. If you want to be an
executive you can't do it. Homelessness interferes with work
– work then interferes with your social life – it's a vicious
circle.'

Lack of easy access to a telephone is also relevant:

'I have a massage qualification from Churchill Centre and
an English language teaching qualification from
International House. I'd love to have a room and a telephone
so that I could combine these and begin to manage my life
properly.'

Interestingly three actresses were interviewed who all strongly responded to this question: they described the theatre as a male-dominated world within which they had had insecure and chequered careers. Lack of secure housing was a large part of this: unlike many of their colleagues they had never been able to obtain a mortgage.

'The more I think about it the more I realize the effect being
homeless has. It makes you feel so unstable and as a
performer it absolutely erodes your confidence. When you're
away on tour it's hopeless if you've got nothing to come back
to.'

Women living in hostels experienced specific difficulties associated with the accommodation. The difficulty of receiving telephone calls from potential employers or employment agencies, or the stigma attached to hostel living militated against finding jobs. A further difficulty was the lack of available employment in the area where the hostel was. As one woman said: 'People are funny about hostels. If you give your address as Camden Resettlement Unit they turn you down'. The sentiment of many was: 'I can't get a job 'til I get somewhere proper to live and I can't get somewhere to live 'til I get a job' – a vicious circle. Women also referred to the difficulty of working or looking for work when such a significant area of their lives was insecure or disrupted. They mentioned feeling insecure, low, unstable, lacking concentration and, as one woman so aptly described: 'It generally depresses you – so you haven't got any get up and go'.

Finally, employment which provides accommodation is a significant aspect of the housing-employment, homelessness-unemployment connection. As discussed earlier many women choose to enter employment where accommodation is provided as a solution to both their housing and employment difficulties. Yet this in itself can become a double bind. Tied employees spoke of being unable to leave tied employment for untied employment, because they were unable to find suitable alternative accommodation. The low pay associated with much of the work in this sector made saving a deposit to enter private rented/owner-occupied housing impossible. As one nurse said: 'Every time you get a pay rise the rent goes up – you don't see any of it. If you were living out, you'd see the difference but you don't here. The canteen food goes up too.'

Moreover, lack of accommodation makes job mobility for those in tied jobs almost impossible so that frequently tied employees find themselves trapped. Another nurse explained:

'Many times you see jobs you'd like, for instance in industry
– and they don't provide places to live – so you can't apply
and you get stuck here because you have a roof. You can go
from one hospital to another but you're back to square one.'

Labour market position, educational qualifications and housing access

What then are the implications of these employment differences for the women's access or lack of access to housing? With the exclusion of the majority of single people from the local authority sector, the decrease in the private rented stock, and the difficulties women encounter entering the owner-occupied sector, the implications of employment status are clear. Given that single women are largely reliant on obtaining accommodation in the private rented sector, income is obviously a key factor. Deposits are usually required and high rents are often charged, due to the scarcity of accommodation. Even if a homeless woman is fortunate enough to find rented accommodation, if her income is low or if she is unemployed she is unlikely to be able to save enough for a deposit and a higher-income tenant is liable to be favoured by the landlord, whose primary concern is the rental income. Women in hostels are particularly trapped since the high cost of this accommodation militates against women saving. In the owner-occupied sector not only is income crucial, future employment prospects are also relevant. Women who are employed in low-paid unskilled and insecure sectors are extremely unlikely to obtain mortgage finance.

Employment status has yet further implications beyond the three main tenures. If a woman is employed she is likely to be less socially isolated, she has an opportunity to meet people at work who may have her to stay, or who may know of accommodation to rent, or help her with advice or contacts. Even if she has no alternative but to live in a hostel, she will be eligible for admission to up-market hostels which tend to be of a better standard, are longer-stay, and allow greater autonomy. In contrast, an unemployed woman is unlikely to be favoured as a tenant and even less so as a mortgagor, and is liable to be more socially isolated. For her, a direct-access hostel may be the only housing option.

Women also frequently marry men whom they meet at, or through, work. A woman who is unemployed or working as a waitress is unlikely to marry a man who is in a well-paid and professional employment. Since there are marked relationships between tenure and income and social class (Reid, 1977, p.157) there are obvious implications in relation to women's homelessness. If a divorced/separated woman was married to a well-paid professional or skilled man, she is more likely to have been living in owner-occupied property than if she was not. If she was married to a low-paid or unemployed man, she is more likely to have been living in the local authority sector. Once the marriage has broken down unemployment and income status is equally relevant. If an unemployed married woman has qualifications or work experience she will be more able to secure employment on marital breakdown than a woman without these. This, in turn, will mean that she will more easily gain access to the private rented sector either through higher income status and/or increased social contact.

A comparison between the housing histories of the homeless women who had been employed in skilled or professional jobs and the women who had never been employed in these sectors endorses this view. The discrepancies are very stark. In every stage of the women's housing histories more of the professional and skilled workers had lived in owner-occupied property, private rented accommodation or stayed with friends or relatives than the unskilled workers. In contrast, greater numbers of the unskilled workers had lived in local authority housing, and more recently had stayed predominantly in hostels.

It is clear from this analysis, therefore, that the income and employment status of the homeless women had significant implications from both the women's current housing situation and for their housing histories. At the point when a woman loses secure accommodation the housing path she follows is greatly affected by her ability to find employment at that point, to keep the employment she has, or at best find better paid employment. Thus, the fact that more women who were living in direct-access hostels and women's aid were economically inactive at the time of losing their last secure home explains, to some degree at least, why for these women emergency hostels were the only option. Thus, where a woman is currently situated on the home-to-homelessness continuum can in part be explained by her current employment status, and also her employment status at relevant points in her housing history.

We saw earlier that a woman's employment status was affected by the level of her education and training, which in turn was affected by her social history in terms of her marital status, and also by her age. The last chapter showed that in many cases women's homelessness related to their role in the family as wife, mother and daughter. Family membership was not the only cause of homelessness, however. Eviction, problems with the accommodation and social factors were also important. What we have seen in this chapter is that what happens to women once they become homeless, and indeed what is the pattern of their housing histories before the onset of homelessness, is directly affected by their position in the labour market at the relevant time.

In terms of a framework which locates women's homelessness within an analysis of patriarchal and capitalist relations, these last two chapters have shown that family structures can give rise to homelessness which then takes different forms depending on the relation of the individual to the labour market. Moreover, there is an articulation between family and class relations and the two cannot easily be separated. A woman's marital and parental status affect her labour force participation which in turn affects her level of autonomy and independence within and outside marriage. Income and employment position also affect women's ideal housing tenure and the strategies which they pursue to find accommodation. These are two of the issues which are taken up next.

CHAPTER 9

Where to now? Housing preferences and strategies

Optimistically we might hope that homeless single women do not stay homeless for ever. The evidence suggests otherwise: without a restructuring of the housing market low-income single households, and women particularly, will remain marginalized, be it living in a hostel or staying with friends. Whatever its form, single female homelessness is intricately related to a housing system where owner-occupation and the family household are key features.

Nevertheless it seems appropriate that we should address the question of what kind of housing homeless women ideally want, and more realistically, what strategies the homeless women had pursued to find accommodation and the nature of constraints confronted. Given the marginalization of single people and women specifically in the housing market, we would not expect a high level of success in obtaining accommodation. Nevertheless the processes of applying for housing and the institutional responses that women encountered illustrate many of the trends discussed earlier. Further, these processes once again highlight differences between the homeless groups which provide further evidence of the heterogeneity of the female homeless population, and of the need to relate women's homelessness to the family and to women's economic position.

Ideal housing tenure and household information

It is important to recognize that individual's expressed preferences tend to be confined to possibilities they consider realisable, or to what is available, and do not necessarily reflect ideal notions or objectives. When questioned as to their ideal accommodation, women who have been living in institutions for a long time are inclined to set their sights very low:

'I'd like a pleasant hostel . . . a hostel with a room of your own and your own key. I'm tired of sharing a dormitory.'

'I'd like a bedsitter with my own kitchen, either furnished or not. That would be plenty for me now.'

In part such statements reflect a realistic assessment of available options. But they also show how these women have themselves absorbed the ideology that condemns single people, especially the notion that single people do not deserve standard forms of accommodation.

More than half the women wanted to live alone; 17 per cent wanted to live with a husband/boyfriend or children or both and 23 per cent wanted to live with friends. Fewer women from the direct-access hostels (44 per cent) wanted to live alone than from the other groups. This can be explained by long periods of institutionalized living and a fear of being unable to cope with living alone. Of the women interviewed, 118 specified their ideal housing tenure: the remaining forty-four responded to the question with indifference and scepticism. Again there are several differences between the women which need to be explained. First nearly half in each of the groups except the women in the up-market hostels wanted a council tenancy. Only one woman in this other group specified this as her preference. This difference seems to be directly correlated with two factors. One is that women who had lived in a council tenancy at some juncture appeared to be more likely to choose this as their ideal[1], (no up-market hostel women had ever lived in local authority accommodation). Second, up-market hostel women did not see council housing as an option due to the lack of rehousing policies in these hostels. In contrast, they were more likely to express a preference for the owner-occupied sector, which reflects their higher income and employment status.

The reasons given for a preference for owner-occupied housing matched widely held notions associated with owner-occupation (Merrett, 1982) – security, freedom, control and financial investment:

'I'd like a place that I owned – it's yours and you've got that security and you can alter it inside as you like, and you know if you do improvements they're yours. You can pass it on to your kids. Landlords don't bother and you just end up doing it for them.'

The most popular form of accommodation articulated by the women was a self-contained unfurnished flat. Since many homeless women have furniture scattered in different places and have lived with furnishings not of their choice for a long time, an unfurnished place is an important criterion:

'I want to find somewhere I can put my furniture – my bedroom suite and my three piece suite. At the moment it is all with my friends. My cat is still with my husband. I miss my cat's company. I'd like an unfurnished council place, alone.'

This desire to regain control over the interior domestic space reflects once again the traditional domestic division of labour, and the significance of the 'home' for women. Another housing preference that some women specified, despite its rarity as a form of housing provision, was some type of shared housing, ranging from group homes – where most facilities and domestic arrangements are shared – to an individual unit of accommodation within a block of other such units, with some communal facilities:

'I'd like to have control over my own space and access to others and communal spaces. I think the whole world should be organized like that – but nowhere is, it's just a dream. . . . I'd like to buy with others too, not on my own, but I don't know how to go about that either.'

The lack of flexibility in allocation systems and in the built stock militates against many women realising this ideal, although some voluntary organizations have established shared schemes for women who want to live with others.

Many of the women believed their ideal housing preferences were 'just a dream', and were realistic about what their options were, aware of the mismatch between these and their ideals. Several, however, responded with their fantasy such as: 'I'd like a pink cottage in the country with roses' or 'I'd like a mansion'.

151

Knowledge of housing rights and council's obligations

We wanted to examine the extent to which the women were unaware of how the housing system, particularly the public sector, operated, since lack of knowledge of the system obviously militates against successfully obtaining rehousing. The general impression we received was one where a considerable lack of knowledge of the housing system was the norm. We would expect that women who had been married would have had less experience obtaining housing in their own right than women who have never married. This indeed proved to be the case:

> 'I didn't know about these places (housing departments, housing associations etc.) until after my husband left me. I didn't even know about the social security. The last four years I've discovered about the other side of life. I haven't been to the council because I'm told you need to be in an area for a certain length of time to qualify.'

However this lack of familiarity with the public sphere, was not only confined to the women who had been married. As one never-married women explained:

> 'I've no idea how to find somewhere, except the housing place, and I don't know where that is. I went there once, years ago when I'd returned to London from a seasonal job at the seaside, and they said they didn't do furnished rooms, they just did flats. So I didn't go back. . . . I could never afford a flat.'

Again the employment status – housing connection is revealed. The more marginalized the women were from the labour market, the less they appeared to know their housing rights. Thirty-five per cent of the women who currently had an income over £60 a week had some idea of the council's housing obligations as opposed to 14 per cent of those women living on state benefit. Likewise, women who had been employed in professional and skilled jobs were more aware of their rights than the unskilled women.

However, employment and educational status was not the only factor. Many more of the concealed homeless and women's aid women knew their housing rights (minimal as these were), which appeared to be a direct result of the efforts made by the staff of the agencies concerned to inform the women. Up-market hostels and most direct-access hostels seldom make an effort to provide such information.

Finally, when the women were asked to explain the lack of housing provision for single people, they invariably referred to the centrality of the family to housing access, and in particular to the necessity of having a child to obtain housing:

> 'Get yourself pregnant and you'll get a flat quick! Lots of girls I know did that, but then you're tied down. You can't go back to work because you can't get child-care so you've got no money. You shouldn't have to go through all that to get a place to live.'

It is interesting that although many of the women expressed a lack of understanding of how the system worked, they were nevertheless extremely conscious of the ideology and the material realities which serve to marginalize single people, and single women specifically.

Rehousing channels and applications

Rehousing policies vary between agencies. The advice agency through which the concealed homeless were contacted made every effort to find their enquirers permanent housing whereas the up-market hostels in direct contrast, operated no such policies. The staff did not see themselves as having a housing advice role, and many did not consider their residents to be homeless. The direct-access hostels fell somewhere in between these two models and varied very widely amongst themselves. The small voluntary direct-access hostels provided the best rehousing channels and had established their own rehousing programme through managing permanent housing association property, as well as obtaining quotes of public sector tenancies, and encouraging women to apply for housing through normal channels (a much higher proportion of women from these hostels had been to the local housing authority). Similarly, the statutory hostel run by the Supplementary Benefits Commission (where twenty women were interviewed) employed resettlement officers to help the women to find permanent accommodation, while the direct-access hostels, which were run by religious and charitable institutions, did not operate coherent rehousing policies. This was particularly the case in the short-stay hostels where women were told to move on after a specific period of stay, frequently with nowhere to go.

It was clear from the interviews that some women had tried every option, while others had limited their search to one or two channels. Again, notable differences emerged between the women. These related to income and employment status and educational qualifications. Sixty-nine per cent of the sample had applied to a local authority for housing at some point during their homelessness; while others had not applied because they thought that the council would be unable to help them. An approximately equal proportion of women from the different groups had approached the council. The exceptions were the up-market hostel women, which reflected both the women's attitudes towards council housing and the lack of hostel rehousing policies. Similarly, more of these women thought that the council would not help because they would not be considered a priority for housing:

'I'm low priority, I'm salary earning (£85-90 gross a week), I'm healthy, I'm capable, I have no responsibilities in their terms. As far as they're concerned I could go on doing this all my life. They expect you to be nomadic.'

Negative images of public housing, including the lack of personal safety associated with some forms of public housing such as walk-up estates with no lighting (a crucial issue for women) were the main reasons given by the women for not approaching the council: 'I don't want a council place really. I'm frightened of the stairs, lifts and corridors in council flats. The long stairways are frightening at night.' One woman living in an area where the council had initiated single person housing schemes expressed a dislike of such 'special' schemes which had discouraged her from approaching the council:

'I haven't been to the council because I'm not interested in sharing with just anybody, people I don't know. I don't think I'd be able to get a single tenancy, and anyway I don't want to live on my own – I'd rather share with friends I knew before I moved in.'

This woman resisted being defined as having special needs, and having no control over those with whom she lived. Once again we see accepted notions of what is deemed suitable for single people not suiting the people concerned.

Of the ninety-six women who had been to the local authority for housing only fifty-seven were registered on the waiting list at the time of the interview. Some women had been actively discouraged by council officials from signing on: some councils operated restrictive policies such as not allowing women to sign on if they were below a certain age or had an income above a certain level. Other local authorities had residency qualifications which clearly disadvantaged single women who are forced to move between boroughs to find accommodation. In some instances there appeared to be a mismatch between the practices of local housing officers and stated local authority policy, so that even in authorities which claimed not to operate restrictive policies, women were discouraged by housing officers at the desk:

'I have been turned away by Camden housing department, despite the fact that I lived there half my life, and my family, mother and sisters and all my friends live there. They say I have too great an income (£70 per week net) and I am not old or ill enough to go on the list. They mean I am not a psychological or physical wreck. If I was destitute or needed welfare assistance they would house me, but they won't because all I am is a single woman.'

Others had been on local authority waitings lists at some juncture but had let their registration lapse, often because in moving from one place to another they had crossed borough boundaries thereby nullifying their registration. Many women were unaware that moving would entail losing their place on the list. Others were disillusioned with waiting endlessly to no purpose and had let their registration lapse when they realised their chances of rehousing were negligible:

'I'm not on the council list any longer although the council knows my case. I renewed my waiting list card, then let it go. Then I rang up again and renewed it again. About two years ago I went to see them to get a list of places as once you're older you have to do something. The place was full of young mums. I didn't get anywhere as there are no council houses for single people like me. They made me feel like I was begging so I don't go anymore. I haven't been sent a renewal card.'

Others described being treated disparagingly during their visits to the housing department, being referred from one person to another, long waits, and so on. A sixty-six-year-old women who was a caretaker, with badly arthritic feet from an early career as a dancer, described her experience:

'I went to the housing department last year. I told them I'd been on the list in another borough and I thought the points I'd gained there would carry over. But they told me they wouldn't and I'd have to start from scratch again on the list. I had an appointment. I arrived and it was a big empty room. I waited and waited. No one called me at the appointed time so I went up and asked what was going on, giving my name – Carruthers. The woman behind the desk said rudely: "we've already called it", sounding exasperated. It was my fault I hadn't recognized the mumbled "Cruffers", – "Mrs Cruffers or something", the man sitting waiting behind me said they'd called out. I hadn't heard it at all. Without glancing up again the woman behind the desk directed me curtly to "the middle one", her attention already back on her papers. There were three doors in the room so I made for the middle one and there I found myself in the staff toilet-cum-broom cupboard. "No the middle *desk*" – even more exasperated. Silly of me to have expected some privacy while I answered all their questions. I sat down at the desk in the middle of the big waiting room. The woman interviewing me spared ten minutes, "Arthritis!" she exclaimed, when I told her of my feet, "You should see what the others on the waiting list have, we've got 800. It'll be at least 2–3 years before you get housed!" Unfortunately I look so well. The woman interviewing me looked so dreadful and ill. She probably thought I didn't deserve anything. She slammed her papers together and stood up. "Thank-you" I said. I made her look at me "What for?", she said gruffly – I think she suddenly realized how rude and unhelpful she'd been. "For ten

156

minutes of your time", I said. At Christmas a visitor from the
housing department came to see me here. She was very nice
– she said she'd do her best and put me on to the GLC. She
gave me her card and said I could phone her. But I haven't
heard.'

The Housing (Homeless Persons) Act

Several of the women interviewed fell into the 'priority need'
category for housing under the Housing (Homeless Persons) Act
because of old age, mental or physical vulnerability or by being
at risk of domestic violence. Despite being eligible under the
terms of the Act, they had not been accepted for rehousing. A
battered woman described her rejection on two counts: first, the
local authority told her that the women's aid centre constituted a
home, although it was overcrowded emergency accommodation;
and second, the local authority did not define her as being in
'priority housing need' because she had no children. Local authorities tend to vary in their treatment of single battered
women, although refusal to rehouse women in these circumstances is a common practice, and reflects the centrality of
children to obtaining a public sector tenancy. Another woman's
experience illustrates the inherent contradiction associated
with this clause. She was mentally unstable and had been in and
out of mental hospital for some years. With a doctor's report on
the extent of her 'vulnerability' she gained the offer of a council
flat. Having moved into the flat her health deteriorated rapidly,
rent arrears accumulated, and the flat fell into disrepair. Eventually she was evicted and returned to a hostel. This woman was
unable to cope with living on her own, yet because of her mental
state she was rehoused. Those who are not classified as vulnerable, on the other hand, and who would like to live on their own
are not eligible for rehousing. Older women were particularly
anxious about the future having had no success with their local
councils: 'In five years time I'll be 60. I hope I'll have somewhere
by then or they'll put me in an old people's home. That's what
they do to you isn't it?'

Offers of accommodation from the council

Several women had been offered hard-to-let tenancies which they had rejected due to the appalling conditions of the dwelling, lack of public transport, poor environment, or fear for their safety. Since the standard practice is to make homeless people only one offer, these women had been faced with the choice of thoroughly inadequate accommodation or continued homelessness. The following experiences of a forty-seven year old woman illustrate the problems:

'I queued up all night at the GLC – it was a terrible night as I have bad rheumatism. They offered me this place in Lambeth. I went down with my daughter, we thought they must have made a mistake – the door was hanging off, the windows were boarded and it was in a terrible state of repair. the rubbish shute was next door and there was rubbish littered everywhere. There wasn't a curtain in the whole block – broken bottles and tough kids everywhere. It was frightening, really scary and such a long way away from Hackney. I'd rather live in a bus shelter, and my daughter said she wouldn't put her dog in there. My daughter phoned and asked if they'd made a mistake and they said 'no – it was the only offer I'd get and if I didn't take it, that would be it'. I couldn't believe they hadn't made a mistake.'

It is interesting that this woman raised both the issues of the isolation and fear associated with living in this estate and of distance of the estate from where her friends and family lived, indeed from where she too had been living all her married life. Another woman was offered a standard council tenancy in Commerical Road but turned it down because she was working shifts in Piccadilly, reiterating a fear of violence: 'it was too dangerous to walk round there at 11.00 at night – who'd do that – heavens above?'

The private sector and housing associations

Only ten of the women had applied for a mortgage at some point. These women came from the concealed homeless group and from the up-market hostels, and had been employed in skilled or professional jobs at the time of application. None had been successful, either because their incomes were too low, their employment prospects were poor, or they had insufficient capital for a deposit. One woman had decided to live in a hostel for some years while trying to save for a deposit but found that the rise in house prices continually outstripped her ability to save.

A much greater number of women had attempted to find accommodation in the private rented sector, yet even in this sector there were financial constraints: First, the scarcity of private rented accommodation in London means rents tend to be high even for the lower standard dwellings. Second, some flat agencies illegally charge clients for registering on their list or for supplying addresses of accommodation, and the majority require clients to pay a sum of money for accepting a tenancy, which is not an illegal practice (see 'After Six', 1981:50). Third, landlords usually ask prospective tenants for some deposit in advance, which can frequently amount to several hundred pounds. Moreover, several of the black women mentioned encountering racist landlords or estate agents. It is not surprising, therefore, that many women did not consider private rented housing as a viable option. Even those who had been offered accommodation spoke of the offers being unacceptable. Some mentioned the conditions: 'Some accommodation I was offered was so grotty that I went round the corner and cried my eyes out. How do people have the nerve to rent such appalling accommodation?' While restrictions imposed on their behaviour were also prohibitive: 'I was offered a place, but they wouldn't allow my boyfriend through the door.'

Finally, at the 'sharers' end of the market access tends to be restricted to specific types of people, such as 'vegetarian . . . non-smokers . . . interested in astrology . . . ' which excluded the majority of homeless women we interviewed.

Approximately half the total sample of women interviewed had applied to housing associations for permanent housing. Again applications to housing associations related to the level of information given to the women (thus, the largest proportion of women who had applied were from the housing advice agency (75 per cent) which kept and distributed very up-to-date information on housing associations, and the women's employment and income status. (Sixty-five per cent of the women who had had professional or skilled employment had applied to housing associations compared to 29 per cent of the women who had never been employed in these sectors.) The experiences of the women who had applied were remarkably similar. Almost all the women complained of having written letters to housing associations, often to as many as twenty or thirty associations, only to be told that the waiting list was closed or to receive no reply at all:

> 'I got the addresses of over 20 housing trusts and associations from the yellow pages. I was told by the ones I wrote to that they only take people who are in desperate need via the local authority, or that the list was closed, or that I wasn't the right category. The only place that helped was the Church Army Housing Association. I might be offered a bedsit by them. I don't know where or when.'

Hostels and advice agencies

The data on applications to hostels reveal significant differences between the groups in relation to the housing strategies pursued. The most interesting points to emerge are first that the majority of the concealed homeless had never applied to the direct-access hostels. Second, none of the direct-access hostel or women's aid women had applied to up-market hostels and only a few women from the two groups had approached advice agencies. Also most of the up-market hostel women had not applied to direct-access hostels and only 24 per cent had approached an advice agency. From the comment made by the concealed homeless women, it would appear that they were reluctant to live in an institutionalized environment. To many women the notion of hostel living – particularly in direct-access hostels – was imbued with stigma, and represented the worst housing option: 'I couldn't bear to live in one of those places – it would make me feel I'd reached the end of the road, with nowhere further to go.' This view appeared to be shared by the women from the up-market hostels also. Women from direct-access hostels and women's aid centres, on the other hand, were unlikely to apply to up-market hostels; first because they are not advised to do so; second, because they are liable to be excluded on the basis of their income and employment status, and third, because in many cases, they did not know of their existence.

The women who had approached advice agencies for help with

their housing had met with a range of responses. Some advice workers were seen as helpful and kind while others had provided little information or simply handed their enquirers lists of housing associations with no further explanation. The advice agency (After Six) through which the concealed homeless women had been contacted, were the most highly praised: 'They were very kind, they didn't give you the brush off. They were the first people that ever listened' and, 'they were very efficient and helpful which I didn't expect in London'. Both these women expressed what was a common theme – the importance of a kind and helpful response, even if at the end of the day no accommodation could be offered or provided.

The four selected groups of homeless women thus appeared to be relatively discrete in terms of the agencies or institutions they approached for help with their housing problem. The majority of the concealed homeless did not appear to go to hostels, while the majority of hostel women had not approached advice centres and tended instead to be referred to hostels by social workers, housing departments, the police or through friendship networks. There was thus little cross-over between the groups of women in relation to the housing circumstances in which they were situated. This information on housing strategies pursued and housing 'solutions' adopted reinforces the picture which emerged in the last two chapters – that income and employment status, as well as marital status and social networks, affect both a woman's knowledge of the housing system and her eventual position at the homelessness end of the home-homelessness continuum. Moreover, the different policies and practices of the agencies have implications for the women who approach them which further differentiates them. Women who are fortunate enough to contact a helpful advice centre, a small direct-access hostel or a women's aid centre, *may* eventually gain access to rehousing through the channels established by the relevant agency or institution. If on the other hand a woman finds herself in an up-market hostel or a large direct-access hostel, she is most unlikely to move on to a more permanent form of accommodation. In one sense, therefore, these institutions reinforce a woman's homelessness rather than seek – in so far as it is possible – to make her homelessness a temporary period in her housing history. Thus the nature of the institutional response has serious implications for an individual homeless woman's future housing prospects.

CHAPTER 10

Conclusion

We began this book by asking several questions: Does women's housing need or homelessness become concealed through the lack or inadequacy of existing housing provision? How does a framework which incorporates an analysis of the sexual division of labour in a patriarchal and capitalist society help us to understand women's homelessness? Do single homeless women constitute a homogeneous group? Can single female homelessness be defined, and indeed is the term 'homelessness' a useful one? Can we now answer them?

There is a strong case for the argument that an unquantifiable proportion of women's potential homelessness remains concealed. First, there are clear indications of a need for more housing for non-traditional households, particularly single people. Demographic evidence showed a recent and continuing increase in the number of one-person households in the last decade, due to the decrease in marriage rates, the trend towards marriage at a later age, increased longevity, particularly amongst women, and the growing proportion of marriages ending in divorce. If these factors are taken together with changing ideology, where notions of living outside the nuclear family structure, and female independence, are no longer associated with such strong moral stigma, the argument for a growing need for single person housing and housing for women on their own, specifically, is a strong one. Further, if we take into account first, women's inferior economic position and/or financial dependence on a male partner and second, restricted labour market opportunities for women (particularly untrained women in their forties or fifties) we can see that women may be liable to stay in inadequate domestic housing situations because of the lack of available alternatives.

163

Conclusion

A Marxist-feminist analysis provides a useful framework for understanding women's homelessness at several levels. Marxist-feminist accounts of the dominant patriarchal family form can clearly help us understand the centrality of the family household to housing policy and provision. We saw first how the marginalization of non-family households, and single female households in particular, derives from this centrality. And second, how the sexual division of labour within which women's primary role is a domestic one, with consequent implications for their position in the labour market, provides a crucial framework for analysing women's homelessness. The interview material substantiated this position. Many women became homeless through the breakdown of a marital or cohabiting relationship, and had been dependent on their partner for their housing, either materially, financially, or psychologically. When the relationship ended they were not equipped financially, nor in terms of understanding how the housing system worked, to find accommodation. Other women had lost housing through different mechanisms of the patriarchal family structure, having cared for an elderly parent, for example, or having put their housing security secondary to the care of their children. Moreover many women who became homelss were in an inferior economic position, either currently unemployed, or in unskilled employment and consequently low-paid, or in skilled employment where the wages, conditions and future employment prospects were poor. The women's low economic status clearly derived from a lack of further education and training and from their expected roles as housewives and mothers within the family. This status militated against finding accommodation in the private sector – the only option for most single people.

Likewise, although psychological or social factors such as mental illness and childhood upbringing appeared to affect women's access to housing historically, and their current housing situations, an emphasis on such factors was shown to be misplaced. Instead housing problems or the lack of adequate housing exacerbated or brought on the mental problems experienced. Thus we would argue that the centrality of the family to housing was an indirect causal factor in single homeless women's mental problems. Moreover, the housing system is not structured adequately to provide accommodation for individuals who are or have been mentally ill, with the result that some people who are discharged from mental hospitals become homeless. Much of the rhetoric behind this policy of discharging people from mental hospitals is based on the assumption that the family, and women in particular, will provide the necessary care.

Whether or not single homeless women can be said to constitute a relatively homogeneous group is closely related to the question: can single female homelessness be defined? Our starting-point was that it was useful to think in terms of a home-to-homeless continuum, which spanned the breadth of housing situations from outright owner-occupation at one end to sleeping rough at the other. We argued that there was a range of hostel accommodation which housed single homeless women and showed that the focus of homelessness research had tended to be on women using this form of provision. Moreover statutory definitions of homelessness were shown to largely have excluded single homeless people entirely. We also argued that the lack of provision for single women and women's economic and social status meant that concealed homelessness was a significant issue for women, and that a study of single homeless women must include those whose housing need is hidden.

On account of some of the conclusions of the Department of the Environment research, we were concerned with the inherent problems of combining the concealed and the institutionalized homeless and defining them, either implicitly or explicitly, as one homogeneous group. Intuitively we were sure that there would be differences between the women in hostels and the concealed homeless which would explain why they were living in the specific form of accommodation in question. The empirical data confirmed the necessity of locating women's homelessness within an analysis of patriarchal and capitalist relations and of disaggregating homeless groups. Women clearly became homeless for a variety of reasons: marital dispute or the breakdown of other family relationships through dispute or death; eviction, requests to leave, harassment (sexual and/or racial) and dispute in the private rented sector; the loss of employment or ill-health in tied accommodation; arrears in the public sector and the high financial costs in the owner-occupied sector. At the point of losing accommodation, the crucial question is why do some women become homeless, while others are rehoused within a short period of time? Further, of those who do remain homeless, why do some women end up in hostels, while the housing need or homelessness of others becomes concealed?

What the research illustrated very clearly was that a range of factors influence a woman's position on the home-to-homelessness continuum, and that these factors are intricately inter-related. Most significant are the following: a woman's marital background and her housing experiences during marriages, education and training, current and past employment status, family history, age, race, current and past social relationships, psychological state, knowledge of the housing system, and the advice and support that she receives from institutional agencies. The evidence revealed a hierarchy within the sample of homeless women. If a woman had been married, had no qualifications, was unemployed, was in the older age group, knew little of the housing system, and so on, she was much more likely to be living in a direct-access hostel than in an up-market hostel, or staying with friends. On the other hand if a woman was employed and was relatively well-paid, was younger and well-qualified, her homelessness was more likely to be concealed. The women's housing histories revealed similar patterns. Overall, women from the women's aid centres resembled the direct-access hostel women in employment, income, educational, marital and housing status terms, and the up-market hostel women resembled the concealed homeless according to these criteria also; although there were some differences.

These findings suggest two important conclusions. First, if the term 'homeless' is employed to describe the single who are living in hostels as well as the single who are staying with friends or who are living in some form of inadequate or temporary housing, the homeless groups need to be differentiated. If single homeless women in these different housing circumstances are treated as a homogeneous group and if reasons for homelessness are evaluated the conclusions are liable to be tenuous. Similarly, policy recommendations for the single homeless group constructed on an assumption of homogeneity are liable to be misconstrued and thus of little value. Second, given the significant differences between the groups of women who were interviewed, all of whom could be defined as homeless according to current usage of the term, the term 'homeless' is clearly ambiguous and thus not a useful one.

Conclusion

This brings us to the fourth question. In the second chapter, definitions of homelessness and the difficulty of constructing a straightforward definition were discussed. We argued that women's homelessness was particularly difficult to define, because of women's specific relation to the home and their role in the family. This analysis of the problems of conceptualization was substantiated later by the homeless women themselves: many gave contradictory responses defining themselves either as 'not living in a home' and 'not homeless', or as 'living in a home', but also as 'homeless'. Definitions given by the women were constructed on similar premises to our own; that is, that the material conditions, control, social relations, privacy, emotional and physical well-being associated with a dwelling had to be considered. The historical analysis showed that the definitions and conceptualization of homelessness had changed over time, and further substantiated the argument that homelessness was socially, culturally and historically constructed. The second half of the book, based on the interviews with the homeless women, revealed marked differences between the four homeless groups. What then, should we conclude?

The concept of homelessness needs to be reconstructed if not abandoned. To a large extent the difficulties inherent derive from the notion of a 'home' and what that means. As we have illustrated the range of meanings attributed to the home and to homelessness is both too vast and too complicated to have any explanatory or prescriptive use. At present it is employed statutorily in the narrowest possible way to exclude many households who do not have adequate housing in their own terms. Hence the extent of unsatisfactory housing that individuals and households have to tolerate is grossly underestimated by the use of this term. Likewise, if homelessness is used vaguely it ceases to have any meaning and any impact. Yet there is no obvious place to draw the line, since so many aspects of a dwelling are of relevance, particularly to women in their role as domestic labourers, and these change according to the household involved, and the current economic and social climate.

In policy and research terms what is needed is a recognition that material conditions and standards, the need for space, privacy, control, safety, self-expression and physical and emotional well-being, are all important aspects of a dwelling and have to be taken into account. The significance of these will obviously vary across time and space, and also according to the household for which the dwelling is intended. Idealistically, our objective would be to provide a dwelling which satisfied these criteria for every household recognizing that these criteria are relative and socially and culturally determined and hence are not absolute. Only then would homelessness, in whatever sense the term was used, be truly eradicated.

Finally, why has the lack of adequate housing and single female homelessness specifically, not been perceived as a crucial social or economic problem for many years? Why, despite the fact that every measure of housing need and poverty points to a worsening housing crisis, is the seriousness of the situation frequently overlooked? The historical analysis revealed that at various junctures since the Second World War, homelessness or the housing crisis have become a focus for media and public attention only to recede again a short time later. Often this prominence was not related to very specific changes in the housing market or other economic events; nor have statistical evaluations of the extent of homelessness necessarily affected the way it has been perceived. In some respects the media representations or official reactions which suddenly express concern about a dramatic increase in homelessness, or which cause homelessness to be of public concern (for example: 'Cathy Come Home' in 1969), can be described in terms of a 'moral panic' as defined by Cohen (1972, p.28):

> Societies appear to be subject, every now and then, to periods of moral panic. A condition, episode, person or group of persons emerges to become defined as a threat to societal values and interests: its nature is presented in a stylised and stereo-typical fashion by the mass media; the moral barricades are manned by editors, bishops, politicians and other right-thinking people; socially accredited experts pronounce their diagnoses and solutions; ways of coping are evolved or (more often) resorted to; the condition then disappears, submerges or deteriorates and becomes more visible. Sometimes the object is quite novel and at other times it is something which had been in existence long enough, but suddenly appears in the limelight.

Conclusion

Why is it that homelessness specifically so seldom has appeared in the limelight since the early part of the century? One reason lies in the division between the private and public spheres. Despite the existence of public housing the home exists as, and tends to be seen as, privatized – a matter for individual choice and action. The lack of a home is perceived in the same way – the individual household is left to find its own solution. It is interesting to compare homelessness with unemployment, since both a home and employment would, in our society, generally be considered pre-requisites for existence (at least for men, provided that they are able-bodied and below pensionable age). It is suggested here that unemployment is of greater public concern precisely because of the division between the public and private spheres. The workplace, the point of production, is the place where struggles between capital and labour are acted out; it operates within a more public and socialized context, the home does not. Waged labour is organized in a way that domestic labour is not. Thus the recently unemployed are closer to a form of collective organization – notably the trade union, and more recently centres for the unemployed – where their interests may be articulated. Certainly at the point of losing employment, when redundancies are sometimes collectively fought, this is likely to be the case. For the homeless, on the other hand, there is no significant organized resistance; it is only in exceptional cases that others (except friends and families) will struggle with them collectively against an eviction, or be involved at any level. The sexual division is crucial here. It is frequently women who lack the power or time to organize around their housing or homelessness. If they are part of a nuclear family it will be the women who are most directly affected by housing problems, trying to nurture and care for their children, and possibly husband, in difficult circumstances. But due to the isolated nature of the family household, an individual woman within it is often powerless to struggle.

These would appear to be some of the reasons why the trade unions, and other organizations which represent working-class interests, have not taken up homelessness. Also, the stronger sections of the working class, those in secure and well-paid employment, are often not the same members of the working class who become homeless. The homeless are clearly those with few resources, often the lower paid, single-parent families, women and immigrants. These groups are not in such a strong bargaining position and their needs are less easily articulated.

Single homelessness is further compounded by the ideological acceptance of the family norm and by the lack of coherence of non-family and single households as a group, and the consequent lack of visibility of this relatively large section of society. Where single homeless women are concerned this problem is exacerbated yet further by their relegation to the domestic sphere and their lack of economic and political power in the public sphere. Thus, the sexual division of labour reinforces the hidden nature of women's homelessness, which in turn means that the issue is not a central one. Our final point is that the lack of public concern about homelessness also derives from the definitional question. The elusiveness of the term, and its narrow usage by politicians, policy makers, and those responsible for allocating housing, serve in part to contribute to its invisibility. Until there is an adequate notion of what exactly homelessness is, or better still a new conceptualization of the issue which incorporates the kinds of arguments which we have put forward here, homelessness, housing need, or inadequate housing will continue to be largely ignored.

Notes

Chapter 2 Definitions of homelessness

1 The standards set by this committee have now been abolished.
2 Note the prevalent assumption of a male household head.
3 This clause was introduced as a result of pressure from the Women's Aid Federation.
4 Although building societies frequently do not take the whole of a woman's income into account (EOC, 1978).
5 In the NAB (1966) survey of homeless single people sleeping rough, only 6.6 per cent were women. Ten of the women interviewed in direct-access hostels mentioned having slept rough at some juncture.

Chapter 3 Homeless women – an historical perspective, from industrialization to the Second World War

1 The extent to which this economic activity among women was in part a statistical illusion thrown up once statistics started being collected is not clear. The statistics recorded economic activity in terms of regular paid work as close as possible to the model of the factory and so on, while women's more casual and ill-defined work, even when paid, was not recorded. Thus, once women started to become more important as part of the formal and officially recognized workforce, there was the notion that they were entering an economic role which they had not previously played.
2 Note the lack of family/homelessness connection made here.
3 It is interesting to see the prevalence of this concern expressed by the women interviewed.

Chapter 4 Homeless women: an historical perspective: from the Second World War until the early 1980s

1 A 'primary family unit' was defined in the 1951 Census as consisting solely of married couples or widowed or divorced person with their children or certain near relatives (parents and grandparents, or brothers and sisters aged sixteen or over as long as not married, or, if widowed or divorced, not accompanied by children of their own).

171

2 Average weekly earnings of full-time manual women workers aged eighteen or over were 4.49 in 1951 and of similar male workers aged twenty-one and over was 8.30 (DE, 1974, p.61, Table 36).

3 147,000 divorces were granted between 1951 and 1955 as opposed to 199,000 between 1946 and 1950 and 686,000 between 1976 and 1980 in England and Wales (OPCS, 1980, p.12).

4 The National Register of Casuals for England and Wales had 469 new women registered between March and September 1946, rising to 1,091 new cases between July and December 1948.

5 The numbers of people not remarrying after divorce increased from 210,000 in 1951 (130,000 women, 80,000 men) to 600,000 in 1971 (364,000 women, 237,000 men) (CSO, 1978, p.50).

6 In 1968 the average hourly earnings rate of manual women workers over eighteen was 59.55 per cent of the rate for male manual workers over twenty-one (Department of Employment and Productivity, 1971, Table 48).

7 DHSS Circular 21/73 was concerned with making increased provision of beds for alcoholics by funding voluntary projects providing residential accommodation for alcoholics.

8 The London County Council Census of 1964 found only fourteen women sleeping out, and the nightly average of government reception centre beds taken by women in 1960 was only around nine. But by 1971, just after the opening of the new Camden Reception Centre for women, which was in addition to the larger one in Southwark, almost all of the total of 100 beds were taken each night.

9 (Brandon 1971, p.8) *Women 55+*: Loss of heterosexual attraction, older prostitute; depressed and drained – often alcoholic. *Women 30–35*: Often alcoholic; sleeping with men for money and accommodation; prison, night-shelter and lodging house round. *Women 16–30*: Sexual deviation, mainly lesbian, association with drugs.

10 Many women do not register as unemployed because they are not entitled to benefits, do not expect to find employment etc. Hence these figures underestimate 'real' levels of female unemployment.

11 By 1981 there were approximately 11,500 bedspaces left in London.

12 Housing Associations are non-profit making organizations providing rented housing.

13 The Act originated in 1974 as a joint DHSS and DOE circular (18/74) to local authorities asking them to base their policies towards the homeless on three main principles: 1) the transfer of the responsibility for homelessness from social services to housing departments; 2) the provision of accommodation for certain priority groups of homeless people (families with children, elderly etc.); 3) the emphasis was on policy measures to prevent homelessness occurring.

14 Previously homeless families, and others for whom local authorities accepted responsibility, were housed under Part 3 temporary

accommodation of social services departments.
15 Between 1972 and 1977 there was a threefold increase in the number of single person applications to local authority waiting lists (GLC Survey of New Entrants to Waiting Lists – unpublished).

Chapter 5   The family and housing: the marginalization of single households

1   The Law Commission Survey which was discussed in the Finer Report (DHSS, 1974, p.375) found that only 14 per cent of the tenants interviewed had joint tenancies, and in 82 per cent of the cases the husband was the sole tenant.
2   Again this has particular implications for women who are less likely to have acquired these skills – either formally through their education or informally at home from their parents or from friends.
3   Formerly the casual wards.
4   This confirms Townsend's (1979, p.528) finding that the poorer sections of the population pay the most for their housing.

Chapter 6   Experiences and definitions of homelessness

1   Note the use of the word 'house' not home here.
2   This includes general anxiety states, insomnia, tension, depression and other problems, for which a woman has sought help from a doctor. In most cases she would have simply been prescribed tranquillizers, sleeping pills, sedatives or anti-depressants.
3   For example Orwell's *Down and Out in London and Paris*.

Chapter 7   Womens' housing and homelessness

1   Local authorities have become more constrained in this respect, since the 1980 Housing Act granted security of tenure to council tenants. The problems created by this will be discussed below.
2   Note the use of the word 'home' to describe the country she was brought up in, but has not lived in for twenty-three years.
3   Excluded from the figures are those who were staying in these sectors with friends or relatives.

Chapter 8   Homeless women and the labour market

1   We are using the classification 'skilled' and 'unskilled' in the traditional sense, since these definitions tend to reflect differences in pay, job security, employment prospects etc. Nevertheless definitions of skill do contribute to the lower status of women's employment.

Chapter 9   Where to now?

1   Sixty-one per cent of the women who had lived in local authority housing at some point gave a council tenancy as their ideal, compared to 27 per cent of the women who had not lived in this sector.

Bibliography

The Ada Lewis Women's Hostels (1979), 'Annual Report No. 67', London, Ada Lewis Housing Association.

After Six Housing Advisory Service (1974), 'The First Two Years 1972–1974', London, 'After Six'.

After Six Housing Advisory Service (1978), 'Annual Report, 1978', London, 'After Six'.

Austerberry, H. and Watson, S. (1982), 'Women's Hostels in London', London, SHAC.

Austerberry, H. and Watson, S. (1983), *Women on the Margins*, London, City University Housing Research Group.

Austerberry, H., Schott, K. and Watson, S. (1984), 'Homeless in London 1971–1981', London, ICERD, London School of Economics.

Bahr, H. (1973), *Skid Row – an introduction to disaffiliation*, Oxford, Oxford University Press.

Barrett, M. (1980), *Women's oppression today. Problems in Marxist feminist analysis*, London, Verso Editions and NLB.

Barrett, M. and McIntosh, M. (1982), *The Anti-Social Family*, London, Verso and NLB.

Batten, D. (1969), in Cox, *et al. The Rink Report*, London.

Beales, H.L. (1949), 'The Victorian Family', in Harman, Crisewood (ed.) *Ideas and Beliefs of the Victorians*, London.

Beauvoir, S. de (1949) *The Second Set*, Harmondsworth, Penguin.

Beechey, V. (1978), 'Women and Production: a critical analysis of some sociological theories of women's work', in Kuhn, A. and Wolpe, A., (eds) *Feminism and Materialism*, London, Routledge & Kegan Paul.

Beirne, P. (1977), *Fair Rent and Legal Fiction*, London, Macmillan.

Berry, M. (1981), 'Posing the housing question in Australia: Elements of a theoretical framework for a Marxist analysis of housing', in *Antipode*, vol.13, no.1.

Booth, C. (1898), 'Common lodging houses', in *Life and Labor of the People of London*, vol.1.

General Booth (1970), *In Darkest England and the Way Out*, London, Charles Knight and Co. Ltd. (First published, 1890, Salvation Army).

Booth, B., Mrs (1979), 'The need for real homes for women: National Conference on Lodging-House Accommodation for Women', (London,

1911), quoted in Davidoff, L., 'The separation of home and work. Landladies and Lodgers in Nineteenth and Twentieth Century England', in Burman, S. (ed.), *Fit Work for Women*, London, Croom Helm.

Bowley, M. (1945), *Housing and the State, 1919–1944*, London, Allen & Unwin.

Bowley, R. (1949), 'Women in a man's world', Bureau of Current Affairs, London, Carnegie Trust.

Brandon, D. (n.d.), 'The decline and fall of the common lodging house', London, Christian Action Publications.

Brandon, D. (1969), 'The Treadmill – a report on the common lodging house', London, Christian Action.

Brandon, D. (1970), 'Homeless alcoholic women', London, Christian Action.

Brandon, D. (1971), 'Women without homes', London, Christian Action.

Brandon, D. (1973a), 'Homeless in London', London, Christian Action.

Brandon, D. (1973b), 'A community for homeless women', *Social Worker*, 16 June.

Brandon, D. (1974), 'Guidelines to research in homelessness', London, Christian Action.

Brown, G. and Harris, T. (1970), *Social origins of depression*, London, Tavistock.

Bruegel, I. (1978), 'What keeps the family going?', *International Socialism*, vol.2, no.1, quoted in Barrett, M., *Women's oppression today. Problems in Marxist feminist analysis*, London Verso Editions and NLB.

Bruegel, I. (1983), 'Women as a Reserve Army of Labour: a note on recent British experience', in Whitelegg, *et al.* (eds), (1983), *Changing Experiences of Women*, Oxford, Martin Robertson.

Burman, S. (ed.) (1979), *Fit work for women*, London, Croom Helm.

Butler, J.E. (1896), 'Personal reminiscences of a great crusade', quoted in Sigsworth and Wyke, 'A study of Victorian prostitution and venereal disease', in Martha Vicinus (ed.), *Suffer and be Still, Women in the Victorian Age*, London and Bloomington, Indiana University Press.

Byrne, E. (1978), *Women and education*, London, Tavistock.

Camberwell Council on Alcoholism (eds) (1980), *Women and alcohol*, London, Tavistock.

Cambell, B. and Charlton, V. (1978), 'Work to Rule – Wages and the Family', *Red Rag*.

Caplow, T. (n.d.), 'Homelessness', in Sills, D., (eds) *International Encyclopaedia of the Social Services*.

Castells, M. (1978), *City, Class and Power*, London, Macmillan.

Census of Great Britain, (1851), 'The numbers and distribution of the people, their ages, conjugal condition, occupations and birthplace', London, Longman, Brown, Green and Longmans.

Census of Great Britain (1931), 'Housing report', London.

Central Housing Advisory Committee (1951), *Housing for Special Purposes*, London.

CHAR (1975), 'Homes not institutions for the single homeless: a CHAR policy statement', London, CHAR.

CHAR, (1977), 'Standards of accommodation for Single people', by D. Ormandy and A. Davies, London, CHAR.

CHAR, The Campaign for Single Homeless People (1980), 'Report from CHAR National Housing Conference', London, CHAR.

Chesterton, C., Mrs (1928), *In Darkest London*, London, Stanley Paul and Co. Ltd.

Children's Employment Commission (1864), CEC 2nd Report, London.

City of Peterborough (n.d.), *Municipal Tenants Handbook*, Gloucester, British Publishing Co. Ltd.

Cockburn, C. (1983), *Brothers, Male Dominance and Technological Change*, London, Pluto.

Cohen, S. (1972), *Folk Devils and Moral Panics*, London, Macgibbon and Kee.

Cowley, J. (1979) *Housing for People or for Profit?*, London, Stage 1.

CSO (1970), *Social Trends No. 1*, London.

CSO (1978), *Social Trends No. 9*, London.

CSO (1981a), *Economic Trends, 1982*, London.

CSO (1981b), *Social Trends No. 12*, London.

CSO (1983), *Social Trends No. 14*, London, p.29.

Davidoff, L. (1979), 'The separation of home and work? Landladies and lodgers in Nineteenth and Twentieth Century England', in Burman, S., (ed.) (1979), *Fit Work for Women*,London, Croom Helm.

Department of Education and Science (1965), *Statistics of Education*, London.

DE (1974), *Women and Work: a Statistical Survey*, London.

DE (1975), 'Women and Work. A review', Manpower Paper No. 11, London.

DE (1980), *British Labour Statistics*, London.

DE (1981), *Family Expenditure Survey*, London.

DE and OPCS (1983), 'Enquiry into the structure of personal income taxation and income support, non working women', unpublished, London.

Department of Employment and Productivity (1971), *British Labour Statistics Historical Abstract 1886–1968*, London.

Department of Health and Social Security (1974), 'Report of the committee on one-parent families (The Finer Report)', Cmnd 5629, London.

Department of Health and Social Security (1975), 'Report of the proceedings of a meeting held on 13th March 1975, to discuss research into the needs of homeless single people', London, DHSS.

Diamond, G. (1975), *Alone with no home*, London, Centrepoint.

DOE (1971), 'Fair deal for housing', Cmnd 4728, London.

DOE (1972), *Housing and Construction Statistics*, London.

DOE (1973), *Better Homes: the next priorities*, London.

DOE (1976), *Housing for Single Working People: Standards and Costs*, Circular 12/76, London.

Bibliography

DOE (1977), Housing Policy: A Consultative Document, Cmnd 6851, Technical Volume, London.

DOE (1978), *National Dwelling and Housing Survey*, London.

DOE (1978, 1979, 1981a), *Local Housing Statistics*, London.

DOE (1981a), *Housing and Construction Statistics 1970-1980*, Cmnd 8175, London.

DOE (1981b), *Single and Homeless*, London.

DOE (1982a), *Homeless Households*. Reported by Local Authorities in England, results for second half of 1981, Supplementary Tables, London.

DOE (1982b), 'Statement of government conclusions on the Review of the Housing (Homeless Persons)', Act 1977, London.

Dominion, J. (1982), 'Families in Divorce', in Rapoport, *et al.* (eds) 1982.

Drake, *et al.* (1981), *Single and Homeless*, London, DOE.

Duncan, S. (1976), 'The housing crisis and the structure of the housing market,' Working Paper, Brighton: University of Sussex, Department of Urban and Regional Studies.

Equal Opportunities Commission (1978), 'It's not your business: It's how the society works – The experience of married applicants for joint mortgages', Manchester, EOC.

Francis, S. (1980), 'New women, New Space: A Feminist critique of building design', MA Thesis submitted at the Royal College of Art, May.

Funnell, M. (1973), 'Designing special accommodation – single workers', *Housing Review*, May-June, 1973.

Gauldie, E. (1974), *Cruel Habitations: A History of Working-Class Housing 1780—1918*, London, Allen & Unwin.

Gavin, G., Veroff, J. and Field, S. (1960), *Americans View Their Mental Health*, New York, Basic Books.

Gavron, H. (1968), *The Captive Wife*, Harmondsworth, Penguin.

Ginsburg, N. (1979), *Class, Capital and Social Policy*, London, Macmillan.

Girls Friendly Society (1878), Report of meeting held in October 1878. Mrs Brook Hudson 'A plea for Girls Friendly Lodge in Holborn'.

Glastonbury, B. (1971), *Homeless Near 1000 Homes*, London, Allen & Unwin.

Goffman, I. (1961), *Asylums*, Harmondsworth, Penguin.

Gover. G. (1971), *Sex and Marriage in England Today*, London, Nelson.

Gray, F. (1931), *The Tramp. His Meaning and Being*, London, Dent.

Gray, F. (1979), 'Consumption: council house management' (Chapter 8). In Merrett, S. *State Housing in Britain*, London, Routledge & Kegan Paul, 1979.

GLC (1981), GLC Housing Strategy and Investment programme. Analysis of 1980 London Borough and GLC Submissions, London, GLC.

GLC and London Boroughs Association, (1975), Second Report of the GLC and LBA Working party on the Provision of Accommodation for Single People. London, GLC and LBA

Bibliography

GLC and London Boroughs Association (1981), *Hostels for the Single Homeless in London*, London, London Boroughs Association.

Greve, J. (1964), *London's Homeless*, London, Bell, G. and Sons Ltd.

Greve, P. and Greve, S. (1971), *Homeless in London*, Edinburgh, London, Scottish Academic Press, p.16.

Hansard, (1971), 'Single homeless people', Debate on motion for adjournment, Hansard, vol.820, no.169, London, June.

Hicks, F. (1894), 'Factory girls', in Reid, A., (ed.) *The New Party*, London.

Higgs, M. and Hayward, E. (1910), *Where Shall She Live? The Homelessness of the Woman Worker*, London, P.S. King and Son.

Himmelweit, S. and Mohun, S. (1977), 'Domestic labour and capital', *Cambridge Journal of Economics*, vol.1.

Hodgetts, C. (ed.) (1971), *A Hole Where a Home Should be*, London, Christian Action.

Holcombe, L. (1977), 'Victorian wives and property: Reform of the Married Women's Property Law, 1857–1882', in Vicinus, M. (ed.), *A Widening Sphere, Changing Roles of Victorian Women*, London, Methuen.

Holmans, A.E. (1983), 'Demography and housing in Britain: Recent developments and aspects for research', London, Social Science Research Council.

Home Office (1971), *Habitual Drunkenness Offenders*, London.

Homeless Action and Accommodation (1977–8), *Annual Report*, London, Homeless Action.

Housing Advice Switchboard (1981), *London's Neglected Homeless*, London, HAS.

Humphries, J. (1976–7), 'Women: scapegoats and safety valves in the Great Depression', in *Review of Radical Political Economics*, vol.8, no.1, pp.98–121.

Jephcott and Smith (1962), *Married Women Working*, London, Allen & Unwin.

Laidlaw, S. (1956), *Glasgow Common Lodging Houses and the People Living in Them*, Glasgow, Corporation.

Laslett, P. (1972), 'Mean household size in England since the sixteenth century', in Laslett, P. and Wall, R. (eds), *Household and Family in Past Time*, Cambridge University Press.

Leevers, M. and Thynne, P. (1979), *A Woman's Place, Family Breakup and Housing Rights*, 2nd edition, London, SHAC.

Liddington, J. and Norris, L. (1978), *One Hand tied Behind Us. The Rise of the Women's Suffrage Movement*, London, Virago.

Local Government Board (1872–3), Report of Conference on Poor Relief, Metropolitan Guardians, App. A, no. 3, London.

Magri, S. (1972), *Politique du Logement et Besoins en main d'oeuvre*, Paris, Centre de Sociologie Urbaine.

Mason, N. (1888–9), 'How working girls live in London', Pt. III in *Girls Own Paper*, London.

Mayhew, H. (1851), *London Labour and the London Poor*, London.

Bibliography

McDowell, L. (1983), 'Towards an understanding of the gender division of urban space', *Environment and Planning D: Society and Space*, vol.1, no.1.

Merrett, S. (1979), *State Housing in Britain*, London, Routledge & Kegan Paul.

Merrett, S. (1982), *Owner Occupation in Britain*, London, Routledge & Kegan Paul.

MHLG (Annually), *Housing Statistics for Great Britain*, London

MHLG (1953), *Houses: the next Step*, Cmnd 8996, London.

MHLG (1955), *Report for 1950/51 – 1954*, London.

MHLG (1956), *Report for the Year 1955*, London.

MHLG (1957), *Report for the Year 1956*, London.

MHLG (1961), *Homes for Today and Tomorrow*, London, Report of the Parker Morris Committee.

MHLG (1965), *The Housing Programme 1965 to 1970*, Cmnd 2838, London.

MHLG (1968), *Old Houses into New Homes*, Cmnd 3602, London.

Mill, J.S. (1849), *Principles of Political Economy, with some of their applications to social philosophy*, vol.2, London, Parker.

Ministry of Health (1930), Report of Department Committee on 'Relief of the casual poor', July, London.

Ministry of Labour (1947), *Economic Survey*, Cmnd 7047, London.

Ministry of National Insurance (1954), *Reception Centres for Persons Without a Settled Way of Living*, Report from the National Assistance Board, London.

Ministry of Reconstruction (1945), *Housing*, Cmnd 6609, London.

Mowat, C.L. (1961), *The Charity Organisation Society 1869–1913, Its Ideas and Work*, London, Methuen.

NAB (1966), *Homeless Single Persons*, London.

National Council for the Single Woman and her Dependents (1979), *The Loving Trap*, London, NCSWD.

National Union of Teachers/Equal Opportunities Commission (1980), *Promotion and the Woman Teacher*, Manchester, NUT/EOC.

Norris, M. (1974), Report on Single Homelessness in Surrey, Surrey Community Development Trust, Research Paper, no.8.

OPCS (1968), 'A survey of women's employment', Audrey Hunt, Volume 1 Report, Volume 2 Tables, London.

OPCS (1980), 'Marriage and divorce statistics', England and Wales, London.

Orwell, G. (1933), *Down and Out in Paris and London*, London, Gollancz.

Otto, S. (1980), 'Single homeless women and alcohol', in Camberwell Council on Alcoholism.

Pahl, J. (1980), 'Patterns of money management within marriage', *Journal of Social Policy*, 9.

Parliamentary Papers (185203), LXXVIII, Common Lodging House Act, Report to the Secretary of State for Home Department, London.

Phillipson, C. (1981), 'Women in later life: Patterns of control and subordination', in Hutter and Williams (eds) *Controlling Women. The Normal and the Deviant*, London, Croom Helm.

Phizacklea, A. (1982), 'Migrant women and wage labour: the case of West Indian women in Britain', in West, J. (ed.) *Work, Women and the Labour Market*, London, Routledge & Kegan Paul.

Pickvance, C.G. (1976), 'Housing, reproduction of capital and reproduction of labour power: Some recent French work', *Antipode*, 8, 1:58–68.

Pickvance, C.G. (1980), 'The role of housing in the reproduction of labour power and the analysis of state intervention in housing', in *Housing Construction and the State*, London, CSE, Political Economy of Housing Workshop.

Pincon, M. (1976), 'Les HLM: Structure sociale de la population logée: agglomeration de Paris, 1968', volume 1 Study, volume 2 Tables, Paris, Centre of Sociologie Urbaine.

Quennell, P.C. (1949), 'Mayhew's London', Quennell P. (ed.), Selections from *London Labour and the London Poor*, by Mayhew, H., first published 1851, London.

Ramsay, E. (1979), *Caught in the Housing Trap: Employees in Tied Housing*, London, SHAC.

Rapoport, R. and Rapoport R.N. (1982), *Families in Britain*, London, Routledge & Kegan Paul.

Reid, I. (1977), *Social Class Differences in Britain*, London, Open Books.

Rex, J. and Moore, R. (1967), *Race, Community and Conflict*, Oxford, Oxford University Press for the Institute of Race Relations.

Ribton-Turner, C.J. (1887), *A History of Vagrants and Vagrancy and Beggars and Begging*, London, Chapman & Hall.

Rose, D. (1980), 'Towards a re-evaluation of the political significance of home ownership', in Housing Construction and the State, vol.3, Political Economy of Housing Workshop of the Conference of Socialist Economists, London.

Rowntree, B.S. (1902), *Poverty: A Study of Town Life*, London, Routledge & Kegan Paul.

Royal Commission on Equal Pay (1946), London.

Sandall, R. (1955), *The History of the Salvation Army*, vol.3, 1883–1953, Social Reform and Welfare Work, London, Thomas Nelson and Sons Ltd.

Sandford, J. (1971), *Down and Out in Britain*, London, Secker and Warburg.

SHAC (The London Housing Aid Centre) (1980), *A Decade of Housing Aid, 1970—1980*, London, SHAC.

Shelter Report (1969), *Who Are the Homeless? Face the Facts*, Wilson, D. (ed.), London, Shelter.

Shelter (1972), *The Grief Report*, London, Shelter.

Shelter (1980), *And I'll Blow Your House Down, Housing Need in Britain; Present and Future*, London, Shelter.

Sigsworth, E.M. and Wyke, T.J. (1972), 'A study of Victorian prostitution and venereal disease', in Martha Vicinus (ed.) *Suffer and Be*

Bibliography

Still. Women in the Victorian Age, London and Bloomington, Indiana University Press.

Smart, C. and Smart, B. (1978), *Women, Sexuality and Social Control*, London, Routledge & Kegan Paul.

Social and Community Planning Research (1977), *Interviewers Manual*, London, S. and CPR.

Tidmarsh, D. and Wood, S. (1972), *Report on Research at Camberwell Reception Centre*, London, Institute of Psychiatry, unpublished.

The Times (1891), Letter (partly) on Teachers Salaries, 5 Sept, p.6, col.6.

Todd, J. and Jones, L. (1972), Matrimonial Property (Social Survey Division, Office of Population Censuses and Surveys), London.

Townsend, P. (1979), *Poverty in the United Kingdom*, London, Allen Lane.

Tucker, R.C. (ed.) (1972), *The Marx—Engels Reader*, New York, Norton.

Twining, L. (1876), 'Hives for working bees', (letter) in *Women's Gazette*, vol.1, February.

Vanek, J. (1977), 'Time spent in housework', *Scientific American*, November, pp.116–20.

Vicinus, M. (ed.) (1972), *Suffer and Be Still, Women in the Victorian Age*, London and Bloomington, Indiana University Press.

Vicinus, M. (ed.) (1977) *A Widening Sphere, Changing Roles of Victorian Women*, London, Methuen.

Walkowitz, J. (1977), 'The Making of an Outcast Group: Prostitutes and Working Women in Nineteenth Century Plymouth and Southampton', in Vicinus, M. (ed.), *Suffer and Be Still, Women in the Victorian Age*, London and Bloomington, Indiana University Press. London and Bloomington, Indiana University Press.

Webb, S. and Webb, B. (1909), *Minority Report of the Royal Commission on the Poor Law*, London.

West, J. (ed.) (1982), *Work, Women and the Labour Market*, London, Routledge & Kegan Paul.

Whiteley, S. (1955), 'Down and Out in London – Mental Illness in the Lower Social Groups', *The Lancet*, 17 September.

Wickham, A. (1982), 'The state and training programmes for women', in Whitelegg, *et al.* (eds), *The Changing Experiences of Women*, Oxford, Martin Robertson.

Wilson, A. (1978), *Finding a Voice, Asian Women in Britain*, London, Virago.

Wilson, E. (1977), *Women and the Welfare State*, London, Tavistock.

Wilson, E. (1980), *Only Halfway to Paradise: Women in Post-war Britain, 1945–1968*, London, Tavistock.

Women's Gazette (1877).

Young, M. (1952), 'Distribution of Income Within the Family', *British Journal of Sociology*, 3.

Index